Loves, Hopes, and F

Longman Imprint Books
General Editor: Michael Marland CBE MA

* Cassette available

Loves, Hopes, and Fears

Seventeen stories compiled by
Michael Marland
North Westminster Community School, London

Longman

LONGMAN GROUP UK LIMITED

Longman House, Burnt Mill, Harlow,
Essex CM20 2JE, England
and Associated Companies throughout the world.

This edition first published 1975
Tenth impression 1987

Produced by Longman Group (FE) Ltd
Printed in Hong Kong

ISBN 0-582-23339-9

Contents

Handwritten notes:

1. Jot down immediate impressions of the stories.
   eg. enjoyed parts disliked or disappointing.

2. *impie* attention to stories beginning + ending

3. Do authors manage to get your attention + keep it. DO they leave you in suspense

6. comment on editors paragraph.

The Life Guard

by John Wain

Jimmy is a very strong swimmer, but not much good at anything else — even attracting girls, something which his friend Hopper is always talking about. Jimmy lives in a very small seaside town — one which isn't very popular with holiday makers. One man is trying hard to make the town more successful, and when he hears that fears about the bathing being dangerous are keeping people away, he has an idea. He gives Jimmy a job as Life Guard. Jimmy is pleased to have the job and the responsibility; he is confident as a swimmer, but how can he be more confident about himself?

"Hey, see that one go by?" said Hopper. He leaned forward, staring with all his might through the window of the hut. "The tall one in the white bathing dress?"

"Yes," said Jimmy. He flicked a few times with a duster at the clean paintwork.

"The dress was too small for her, did you notice?" said Hopper. "You could see plenty. *Plenty*."

"I don't give much thought to it."

"Of course, you must get so used to it, it's boring," said Hopper. "You get your chances here, all right."

"I don't give much thought to it."

"All day and every day," said Hopper. He went to the door, opened it and stared after the girl in the white bathing dress. 'I'll wait till she starts sun-bathing, then I'll go and look her over."

"Suit yourself," said Jimmy.

Nobody knew why Hopper was called Hopper. It was neither his surname nor his Christian name. But he had been called Hopper at school, as far back as Jimmy could remember, and he could remember back to pretty well their first day there, at the age of five. And now Hopper was an apprentice and Jimmy was the Life Guard of Red Rocks. Everybody was growing up.

"Girls," said Hopper. "They're all waiting for it. Just waiting for it, they are. I soon found that out, at our place."

"There's all sorts," said Jimmy vaguely. He was beginning to tire of the conversation.

"Nah, there's only one sort," said Hopper. He shot Jimmy a crafty look from under his pimply forehead. "They don't think about anything but boys. They sit around thinking about it till they do half your work for you.'

"How d'you mean, half your work?"

"When you start to soften 'em up," said Hopper in a quiet, husky voice. He gave a quick glance over each shoulder, as if afraid someone would come into the hut and overhear him. "You find they've been thinking about it so much, they're half-way there already." He winked and gave a quiet snigger.

"I think I'll have a swim," said Jimmy. He began to take off his shirt.

"Give the birds a look at that manly torso of yours," said Hopper. "You get a good tan, doing this job."

Jimmy wished that Hopper would not examine him so closely. He took his trousers off and hung them neatly over the back of one of the hut's two chairs.

"Swimming trunks on already," said Hopper.

"What else?" Jimmy asked. "I've a job to do."

"Oh, do me a favour," said Hopper. He sniggered again. "Your job is to walk around and make the birds feel good. You'll never have to rescue anybody."

"I'm going swimming now," said Jimmy. "I have to keep in practice."

"I'm not stopping you," said Hopper.

"Yes, but the hut," said Jimmy. "I have to leave it empty. It's a regulation."

Hopper stopped looking cunning and looked sulky. "You mean nobody's allowed in the hut?"

"Not without me," said Jimmy.

Hopper got to his feet. "What kind of a regulation is that?" he asked.

"One of Mr Prendergast's."

"Oh, *him*."

"He's my boss," said Jimmy. He watched Hopper out and then closed the door of the hut. "Why don't you come in swimming if you want something to do?" he asked.

"I've got something to do. I'm going to find that girl in the bathing dress that's too small for her and see if there's anything doing.'

They parted, Jimmy towards the sea and Hopper along the beach. As he walked briskly towards the water, Jimmy thought briefly about Hopper and the girl. He was quite certain that when Hopper located the girl he would never have the nerve to go up and speak to her. He would just sit himself down, about twenty-five yards away, and look at her and think his thoughts. Hopper had always talked about girls in that way, from the time he was eleven years

3

old, but really he was very shy with them. At least as shy as Jimmy himself, which was saying a lot. Since he had left Red Rocks and gone to be an apprentice in an engineering works, and only came home at weekends and holidays, Hopper had talked about girls more than ever, but Jimmy did not believe the things he said. He knew that Hopper had picked up all those stories from listening to the other apprentices. Hopper would never find a girl to do all those things with; he was thin and flat-chested, he had greasy hair that came down so close to his eyebrows that there was hardly room for his pimples, he had bad teeth, and he was not even clever.

The waves came creaming along the sand towards Jimmy's feet. The day was overcast but not at all cold, and the sea looked green and lush as a meadow. Jimmy ran forward until the water was up to his knees, then dived under and began to swim with strong, easy strokes.

Red Rocks is a struggling little place. Also straggling. A long road leads down to the sea, running straight across the sandhills because there are no trees and nothing to turn aside for, and along this road there are a few houses, some in clusters as if afraid of the lonelines, a few bigger ones sturdily on their own. There is also the High Hat Ballroom, which used to be the Rialto Cinema, and there is Owen's Fish and Chip Saloon. Further up, at the T-junction, there is the older and more settled part of the village. Fifty or sixty houses, two pubs and a red-brick church.

For a hundred years or more, Red Rocks has been trying to establish itself as a summer resort. It has the clean, salt sea, it has fresh Atlantic air, and in the little bay it has a half-circle of smooth pale sand, as elegantly rounded as a child's cuticle. At the northern edge of the bay rises the cluster of rocks that gives the place its name, high enough and rough enough for the adventurous big boys of fourteen and fifteen to climb and shout to one another and feel that they're really climbing something. Yes, the place has the makings of a resort. But no more than the makings.

4

A few visitors come in August, a little shanty town of caravans and tents grows up in the field behind Owen's Fish and Chips, but at the beginning of September it all dies down again. Once that cold wind starts whipping across the sandhills, nobody wants to come near the place. And even in the short season of hot weather, when the sea winks in the sunlight and the rocks feel warm to your hand, most visitors go to the larger resorts down the coast, where there are more amenities. Red Rocks keeps in business by holding prices down, offering simple food and not too many amusements to burn up the hard-earned sixpences that have been put by. The families who take their holidays there are usually lower-income-bracket.

Most people in Red Rocks were pretty well resigned to these facts before Mr Prendergast came. In fact, some of them positively liked things the way they were. The pushing, enterprising young ones had all gone off to the towns anyway, and the older ones liked a quiet life. Even some of the young people found it not too bad. Jimmy Townsend, for instance. You wouldn't have said that anything could worry Jimmy, a strongly built boy with a round face and not too much up top. Most of Jimmy's life, except for the tiresome interruptions of morning and afternoon school, was spent either bicycling or swimming. He would have liked to be a P.T. instructor, but that was just the trouble, you had to have training for that, and to get the training you had to pass your exams and go on a special course, and Jimmy could never get on well enough at school to pass any exams. He just couldn't give his mind to it. So when he turned fifteen he just left school and hung about at home. There wasn't any work to do. Sometimes, in the afternoons, he helped out with a bit of potato-peeling for Mr Owen, or dug the Vicar's garden, but it was a rare week when he earned more than ten shillings, and with his big appetite it cost more than that to feed him for a day. After six months of this, it was clear that the time was coming when Jimmy would have to go away to one of the nearby big towns, and live in a hostel and get a job. And this was what worried him. He didn't want to go away. He liked Red Rocks even in the winter, when the salty wind made his eyes fill with tears and sometimes made him get off his bicycle and push it, against the wind's great roaring weight, down the road to the beach. Even the short, dull winter days, when the cold fog lay still on the water, and all you could hear was the muffled rattle of waves pushing the shingle about, and sometimes the cry of a sea-bird, suited him. Jimmy had plenty of patience; he knew how to wait. He would lean on his bicycle and look at the sea and reckon up how many weeks would have to pass, before he could go swimming.

Swimming was Jimmy's great happiness. He could do any stroke. His arms were so powerful, his big chest held so much air, the salty sting of the water sent his blood racing so fast, that he felt more fully alive in the water than on land. Mr Rogers, the schoolmaster, had made jokes about it. 'One of the larger mammals reversing the evolutionary process,' he used to say of Jimmy. 'Townsend is evolving backwards into a marine animal. If he has offspring, they'll probably be gill-breathers.' And he called Jimmy the Amphibian, taking care to explain the derivation from two Greek words so as to make his joke educational for the class.

Jimmy didn't know what reversing the evolutionary process was, but he took it all in good part and waited for school to end so that he could go swimming. And when he got too old to go to school he went swimming more than ever, to get away from his worried feeling. Even on a winter day he would take a plunge if it wasn't too freezing cold, moving rapidly through the water for ten or fifteen minutes before running out and towelling himself in the lee of the rocks. A seal, people said. He ought to come back to earth next time as a seal. But his father grumbled about the cost of keeping him at home, and his mother said nothing but set her lips and began to make enquiries about a nice hostel for clean-living boys in Barrow-in-Furness or Fleetwood or even as far away as Preston. No wonder Jimmy worried. In a place like that, there would be no sea, no rocks, no sand. He would have to spend all the week working, and do his swimming on crowded Saturday afternoons in municipal baths that stank of chlorine.

That was where Mr Prendergast stepped in, with his Development Group. Mr Prendergast really changed Jimmy's life. He was a young and forceful man in rimless glasses who had opened a pharmacy in Red Rocks to sell sun-tan lotion and denture powder to the visitors, and he wanted a lot more customers. He was always talking about Changing the Image. Red Rocks would begin to thrive straight away if it could only Change its Image. He formed a Development Group because he despaired, and quite rightly, of getting any action out of the old Rural District Council.

One evening Mr Prendergast was over in Morecambe and he got talking to a man in the lounge bar of an hotel. This man told him that visitors stayed away from Red Rocks because the bathing was dangerous. Mr Prendergast pooh-poohed the notion, but the man said that there were dangerous currents that swept people out into the Atlantic. This had happened to three people in one season – about 1920, the man thought – and the fact had been widely mentioned in the newspapers. Ever since then, Red Rocks had been known to everyone in the north-west as a place where it was unsafe to bathe.

Mr Prendergast, his glasses flashing angrily, continued to insist that the idea was preposterous and that Red Rocks was a bather's paradise, and he parted on bad terms with his informant. But as he drove home through the night, he worried about this important part of the Image. It nagged at him all the way home, and just as he was turning into his own gateway he got the answer. A Life Guard. A brawny life-saver to be on duty on the beach every day during the season, and not to leave his post until the last bather had gone. He could have a little hut to keep his things in, and to shelter in when it rained, and the hut could have a flag flying above it with a conspicuous colour and the words "Life Guard". As he stopped the engine and got out of his car, Mr Prendergast even knew

7

who the life-guard would be and how much, or how little, they could get him for. That Jimmy Townsend – he and the job were made for each other. What a piece of luck!

The other members of the Development Group, when Mr Prendergast told them his idea at the next meeting, made only one stipulation: that Jimmy Townsend should go and get a diploma in the approved methods of life-saving. So Jimmy went to Morecambe and took some tests. He swam better than the people who were testing him and got his diploma the first time. The hut was built in June. There was a little delay in getting the flag with the words "Life Guard" on it, so Jimmy's mother embroidered one, and Jimmy fixed it up on a pole himself. Everybody said it looked very nice, and Mr Prendergast and his Group sent out a brochure which mentioned "Excellent Bathing for all the Family. Fully Qualified Life Guard and Swimming Instructor Permanently in Attendance".

Jimmy's father was annoyed at that, and said that if he was going to give swimming lessons to every Tom, Dick and Harry that chose to ask for them, as well as being Life Guard, he ought to get two wage packets. Bur Mr Prendergast said it would keep Jimmy from getting bored, because the bay was perfectly safe and there would be nothing for him to do as Life Guard.

All through that summer, the sea danced for joy and Jimmy swam like a glistening porpoise. He practised until he could stay under water for a minute at a time, and when he broke the surface and came blinking up into the sunshine, water poured off his sleek head and the gulls wheeled and cried as if they had seen a walrus. Wading back for a rest, he felt the sand suddenly warm beneath his feet where the water ended, and the red rocks glowed all June under the hot blue of the sky. In the early summer, nobody came to the beach except at weekends, so for five days on end Jimmy was lord and owner of the sea and the shore, king of birds, master of crabs, director of shells and seaweed. At the highest point to which the tide reached, there was an irregular line of oddments – dried seaweed,

shells, corks, salt-whitened sticks, and man-made rubbish –
which the tide had carelessly pushed in front of it and
abandoned. This line of innumerable weightless objects
stretched out as far as you could see on either side, away
down the beach, and Jimmy could imagine it going round
the whole of England, Scotland and Wales. Every twelve
hours the sea came in and inspected this casual demarcation
line, nudging it here and there, straightening one section
and pushing the next into a curve. It was not only the
sea's frontier, it was Jimmy's. He knew that it would only
last for the summer; in winter, the furious high waves
would come streaming in and the harmless little objects
would be flung far inland, to be scattered by the wind.
But for the summer, it was something Jimmy could share
with the kind sparkling sea. Every time he crossed that
line, going towards the water, he felt his troubles fall away
from him and was conscious of nothing but the strength
and springiness of his body. And every time he crossed it
coming out, with his face towards the straggling village
and the sand dunes, he felt wariness gather round him
like a wet towel.

Not that there seemed to be anything he need be wary
of. Mr Prendergast, on behalf of the Development Group,
gave him his small wage, every Saturday night, and seemed
quite satisfied with the bargain. He did nothing to interfere
with the arrangements, beyond coming down to the hut
one Saturday morning and tacking a typewritten notice
on it. The notice was in capital letters and was protected
from the weather by a sheet of transparent plastic. It announced that swimming lessons would be given free of
charge on application to the Life Guard. Jimmy was
pleased to see himself referred to, in capital letters, as the
Life Guard, and he smiled at Mr Prendergast.

"Give the people any help they seem to want, Jimmy,"
said Mr Prendergast, looking seriously at Jimmy through
his glasses. He was a stout, unsmiling young man and his
fair hair was thinning out. What remained was caught by
the breeze and fluttered gaily as he spoke. "Bring them
into it. Specially the shy ones. Keep a look out for the

ones who look lonely and go up and talk to them. Ask them if they want a swimming lesson."

"Yes, sir," said Jimmy. "If they can't swim here they never will. The water's lovely."

"I must try it myself one day," said Mr Prendergast, turning to walk back to his car. Personally he preferred to give his energy to thinking of ways of increasing his income. Swimming was all right for animals that lived in the water. "If I ever do," he added, "I'll make sure that you're all ready to save me if I get out of my depth." He chuckled good-humouredly and Jimmy produced an answering chuckle.

"Well, keep at it," said Mr Prendergast. "Not that there seems to be much to keep at," he added as he moved away.

"The sea's always there, sir," said Jimmy quickly.

"Yes," Mr Prendergast agreed. "Even if the bathers aren't."

He clambered up the rough stone steps and got into his car. Jimmy felt slightly anxious as he went back into the hut. He hoped Mr Prendergast would not begin to regret that he had made him Life Guard and Swimming Instructor. He looked through the window of the hut: it was ten o'clock and the first visitors were just arriving with their beach balls and picnic baskets. He must find someone among this lot, or among one of these lots one of these days, who wanted to be taught to swim. Or, better still, needed to have their life saved.

Time melted away, between joy and anxiety. Now it was August. The field behind Owen's Fish and Chips held three straggling rows of caravans, from little ones like hen-coops on wheels to immense silvery ones fit to be called Mobile Homes. And in the corners of the field, hiding from the wind behind the thick, sloping hedges, were little rashes of tents, holding their heads up above the trampled grass like clusters of mushrooms. It was high season and the weather was good, so that when all the younger visitors crowded together into the High Hat Ballroom or queued for Owen's Fish and Chips, you would have thought that Red Rocks was a thriving resort at last. But even now the boarding houses were only half full.

One Saturday morning, Jimmy managed to get into conversation with a fat woman who was sitting on the beach by herself. He could see that she had a bathing costume and towel with her and he asked her if she liked swimming. The fat woman said that she liked bathing but she couldn't swim. She just splashed about. This was Jimmy's opportunity and he at once offered to teach her to swim. Two or three lessons, he said, and she's be swimming and then she need never fear getting out of her depth. The fat woman said that she never went out of her depth anyway, and she was too old to start learning to swim now. Jimmy privately agreed with this, but he persisted. There were quite a lot of people on the beach that morning and it would be good publicity if they saw him teaching somebody to swim So he shifted from one foot to the other and bent over the fat woman as she sat on the sand, and said that bathing was much more fun if you could swim, and doctors all said how good swimming was for you, and the lessons would be free of charge. "I'm paid by the Development Group," he urged. "It's a free service to visitors."

He felt a fool, bending over the fat woman, and it annoyed him to see out of the corner of his eye that Hopper was standing a few yards away, watching him and grinning. With Hopper was his younger sister, a scrawny girl of ten or eleven with her hair in a pony-tail. Her name was Agnes and she was always making fun of someone or something. Jimmy had never heard her voice except raised in mockery. He did not remember ever hearing her say anything in a normal tone.

Blushing, he turned his back on Hopper and Agnes, and continued to press the fat woman to let him teach her to swim. It was a sultry day; there was a grey haze over the sea and the sun glared down through a hot mist. Jimmy felt himself sweating.

"I'll just start you off," he said to the fat woman. "Then

11

you can carry on and practise by yourself till you feel ready to go on to the next stage."

To his surprise, the fat woman suddenly gave in and agreed to let him start her off. She gathered up her things and went off to one of the bathing huts to get changed. Jimmy stood waiting, his arms crossed on his chest, trying to look grave and responsible. But he could not help being aware that Hopper and Agnes were coming towards him and Agnes was giggling.

"Is that the best you can do, then?" Hopper asked, grinning and jerking his thumb in the direction of the fat woman. "There's some good-lookers here today. Be a pleasure to hold them up in the water."

"Jimmy's too shy for that," said Agnes in a high affected voice. "He's frightened of girls, everybody knows that."

"She wants to learn to swim," said Jimmy off-handedly.

"Come off it," said Hopper. "She wants to get near a nice young feller and it's her only chance to."

"Jimmy's her last chance," said Agnes. "Last chance Jimmy, last chance Jimmy, oh, oh, oh," she sang to the tune of "If you knew Susie".

"If she starts drowning will you rescue her?" Hopper jeered. "I bet she's like that. Ow, hold me tight, I'm going under," he mimed the fat woman, holding out his arms and writhing to and fro.

"It's too hot to argue," said Jimmy.

"The water'll rise when she gets in," said Hopper. "High tide'll be two hours early."

"Jimmy picked the fattest one on purpose," said Agnes. "He can hide behind her so the girls can't see him in his little briefs."

Jimmy longed for the fat woman to come back. Then he saw her approaching. She wore a flowered one-piece bathing costume and a rubber cap. Her thighs brushed together as she walked. Everything about her was thick and white.

"Here she comes," said Hopper. "Two-Ton Tessie. Get the lifeboat out."

"Right then," Jimmy greeted the fat woman. He smiled at her. She looked nervous. "Let's just get in and get used to the water first," he said.

"It's the first time I've bathed this year," she said tensely.

"You'll find the water very nice," said Jimmy.

"Last chance Jimmy, last chance Jimmy," Agnes sang in the background. "Oh, oh, oh."

Jimmy and the fat woman walked towards the sea. "We'll just do a nice easy breast-stroke," he said to her. It embarrassed him slightly to say the word "breast" to a woman. He kept his eyes carefully to the front. The thundery air seemed to be pressing down on his forehead. When they reached the water, Jimmy ran ahead and lightly ducked below the surface. The fat woman advanced step by laborious step, letting the water creep up her pale thighs. "It's cold, isn't it?" she said plaintively. Finally she sank to her knees, with the water at waist-level, and stayed there.

"Well, here's the first exercise," said Jimmy. "What we do, we take the legs first." He showed her how to rest her palms on the sea-floor and hold her chin up while doing a simple frog-like movement with her legs.

But the fat woman was hopeless. She got down as if she meant to do some press-ups, but she seemed unable to move her legs, and every time a tiny wave splashed round her chin she gasped and threw her head up like a frightened mare.

"Look, kick your legs like this, nice and easy," Jimmy urged.

"I'd rather learn at the baths," she puffed.

"You'll soon get confidence," said Jimmy. He sat down on the sea-bottom, with his head and shoulders out of the water, and looked at her helplessly. He felt sure everyone must be watching them and laughing. Ought he to get hold of the fat woman's legs and show her the movements? He just did not know. Perhaps that was what real swimming instructors did: but the fat woman's legs looked so white and pulpy that to touch them seemed obscene.

They splashed about for another five minutes, getting nowhere at all, and then the fat woman said she was cold and was going to get out and dress. Jimmy splashed by her side and they walked up the beach together with water pouring down their legs and arms.

"You'll soon get the hang of it," he said to her, smiling so that the people could see.

"I'll never swim the Channel, that I do know," she said.

She went off to dress and Jimmy towelled himself inside the hut. The door opened and there were the grinning faces of Hopper and Agnes.

"Hey, you stopped too soon," said Hopper. "She was just getting in the mood."

"Jimmy was frightened even of *her*," said Agnes. Her narrowed eyes were as green as a cat's. She put out her tongue and it was like a thin, poisonous wafer.

"Kindly get out of my hut," said Jimmy, swinging round to face them. Agnes disappeared at once, but Hopper stayed where he was and said, "You used to be able to take a joke."

Jimmy looked out of the window. The beach was fairly full but it could have been much fuller. The sea was a wonderful cool refuge from the sticky, headachy day but there were only a couple of dozen people splashing about in it. At the big resorts, they would be jostling one another in the sea, stepping over each other on the beach. Suddenly he felt as Mr Prendergast must feel. It was just not working. Next summer the Life Guard's hut would be taken down and he, Jimmy, would be sent off to the city and shut up all week in an engineering works. He felt desperate.

"Hopper," he said, "come in and shut the door."

Hopper obeyed. "Want a private talk?" he said. "Don't say anything I might regret."

"I want you to do something for me," said Jimmy. "Stage a little demonstration." His heart was thumping heavily.

"A demonstration what of?" Hopper asked.

"Life-saving."

"I don't know anything about life-saving."

"No," said Jimmy. "But I do."

He had dried himself by now and he began to put his clothes on, turning his back to Hopper. But he could feel Hopper watching him. When he turned round, dressed, Hopper's eyes were small and calculating.

"A fake rescue?" he said.

"No fake. I know how to rescue people and I'd like a chance to show what I can do."

"You've got a certificate, isn't that enough?"

"It isn't. I want to pull off a good big rescue at a crowded time like Saturday or Sunday afternoon, right where everyone can see it. Then they'll know the bathing is safe."

"How will they know the bathing's safe if someone pretends to be drowning?"

"They'll see me rescue him. Then they'll know they're being looked after."

"I see," said Hopper slowly. "Nobody wants to learn to swim, so you want somebody to get into trouble and get rescued so everybody'll see you're a big shot."

"Not somebody. You. I want you to go in swimming, pretend to get into trouble, wave to me and give a shout, and I'll swim out and tow you back to shore."

"What d'you think I am, daft?"

"It'll be no trouble, the whole thing'll be over in ten minutes, and I don't expect you to do it for nothing. There's five quid in it for you."

"Not enough," said Hopper.

"It's more than I earn in a week."

"That's your problem. If I'm going to look a fool in front of everybody, the kind of fool that goes out swimming and can't stay in his depth, I want ten quid at least."

"Ten ...? You won't look a fool, it might happen to anybody to get caught up in a dangerous current."

"It might, but it doesn't. I'd be the first and I'd look a fool. I need five pounds for doing the job and another five for looking a fool, in front of birds and all. You're lucky I don't make it fifteen."

15

"You'll do it then?"

Hopper paused for a long moment and then he said, "Cash down first."

"I can't give you cash down. I haven't got it – I'll have to save it up and it'll take me the whole season."

"How much have you got?"

"Three-ten."

"Right, give me that and an IOU for the rest."

He tore a page from his notebook and showed Jimmy how to write out an IOU. "You've got to pay me now," he said. "I can take you to court if you don't. And what about the three-ten?"

"I've got it at home. You can have it tonight."

"Right."

"But you must do the job tomorrow afternoon."

"Right."

Jimmy waited a long time on Sunday afternoon before Hopper came down the road and on to the beach. Hopper was carrying a towel but no bathing costume.

"Are you ready to go in?"

"Yes," said Hopper. "Don't be so anxious. I've got my trunks on under my clothes. Let me come in the hut and change."

"You'd better go to one of the cubicles like everyone else. It'll look funny if you don't."

"All right."

Changed, Hopper looked thin, a pathetic land animal with small blue veins in his legs.

"Let's get it over," he said, shivering already in the cool breeze.

"I've got it worked out," said Jimmy. "We'll go in together and swim out till I say. Then we'll stop and I'll swim back to the shore. You wait a bit, then go out a bit further, and when you're not too close to anyone else, wave your arm and shout for help. I don't want anyone else rescuing you."

"No," said Hopper, "else they'd have to give me ten quid too, wouldn't they?"

He grinned derisively, then looked miserable again. "Oh, let's get it over. I hate the bloody sea."

"You do bathe sometimes. I've seen you."

"Well, I wasn't going to bathe today, so let's get it over."

They walked into the sea, pretending to chat like two friends. When the water came up to waist-level, Jimmy got down and began to swim.

"Come on," he said.

"It's cold," said Hopper sourly. He stood with the water lapping his bathing shorts, as if he was beginning to have second thoughts about the whole thing.

Jimmy swam round him in a circle. "Come on, think of the ten quid."

"That's safe anyway. I've got your IOU."

"But you wouldn't,' said Jimmy. "You wouldn't be a rotten cheat."

"What are you being? Faking a rescue."

"It's not a fake. It's a demonstration. If you don't do it I shan't give you the ten quid and I don't care what they do to me."

Hopper suddenly flopped into the water and began to swim slowly and clumsily. Jimmy swam beside him at the same pace. They went on in silence for a few minutes and then Jimmy said, "Right, stop."

Hopper let his feet down to the bottom and stood on them. The water came up to his nipples.

"A bit further on," said Jimmy.

"No," said Hopper. "This is as far out as I'm going."

"Don't be silly. You can't look as if you're in trouble when you've got your head and shoulders out of the water."

"Well," said Hopper. He considered. "I'll wait here while you go back to the shore and then I'll swim a bit further out and call for help from there."

"All right," said Jimmy. "Only do a good job. Think of the ten quid."

"I ought to have said twenty."

Without answering, Jimmy swam back to the shore and stood up with his feet still in the water. Folding his arms, he walked up and down for a few moments, swivelling his head and body in a leisurely, graceful way so as to survey the whole scene. He conveyed that the bay was his province and that he wanted to be satisfied that everybody was safe and having a good time. The salt water ran down his tanned body and began to dry off. He was covered with a very fine dust of greyish-white salt, as delicate as the pollen-dust on a nettle.

The sea was dotted with heads where people were swimming about. Here and there, little groups stood in the water; parents and two or three children, sometimes swinging the youngest child up and down by its wrists so as to duck it in and out of the water; squealing and gaining confidence. Red Rocks was a wonderful place to spend a happy day. As a resort it was surely coming into its own. Long-legged boys crawled up and down the rocks, imagining themselves in wonderful danger, and two ice-cream vans were selling fast.

Jimmy counted a hundred, quite slowly, before he even allowed himself to look out to sea in Hopper's direction. Hopper was standing in the water, exactly where he had been. When he saw Jimmy look towards him he began to swim slowly away from the shore, turning his head every few strokes to see if Jimmy was watching. Jimmy pretended not to be looking at Hopper, turning his head slightly away from him but keeping his eyes steadily on his slowly bobbing head. This was it. At any moment, Hopper's arm would go up and his cry for help would come to Jimmy across the water.

Jimmy turned once more, moving his feet and going round in a complete circle. The Life Guard's hut stood proudly at the upper edge of the beach, a sign that Red Rocks meant business and that there was enough work there for any honest young man who had no wish to go off to the city and be apprenticed and live in a hostel. As Jimmy's eyes rested on the hut, Hopper's sharp cry came suddenly to his ears. *"Help."* It was a single, high stab of sound. If Jimmy had not been listening for it he would probably never have heard it among all the other sounds that littered the water, the laughter and the shouts of children and the insistent barking of a small dog that ran along the beach. But he did hear it, he whipped round and there was good old Hopper with his arm up, waving. None of the other bathers seemed to have noticed Hopper's distress signals, but that did not matter. He, Jimmy, the Life Guard, had noticed them. He ran forward for a few yards, then did a running dive into the water and began to swim fast, cutting past family groups and a fat pale man floating on his back in striped trunks.

Jimmy swam easily, saving his strength for the rescue, but still nearly at racing speed. He did not want Hopper to have time to get tired of pretending and let his feet down to the bottom. That would make them both look ridiculous. He kept his eyes on Hopper and presently he saw the arm go up again. Then Hopper's head disappeared, for a second or two, right under the surface. Good, he was making a real, convincing job of it. Jimmy increased his speed, taking great controlled breaths every time his mouth came clear of the water. Soon have him out of that now.

As he swam on, he realised that Hopper must be further out than he had seemed to be, from the shore. It was taking him quite some time to reach the spot. Jimmy increased his speed again, going full out now, his heart pounding with effort and excitement. For a few strokes his head was under water, and when he lifted it again he saw that he was quite close to Hopper. Then he saw the expression on Hopper's wild white face. It made his inside go cold.

Hopper's eyes were turned upward as if help might come from the sky. He did not see Jimmy close to him, but took a great struggling gasp and shouted up into the air.

"Drowning..."

Water slopped into his mouth and he coughed and went down again.

"Hopper," Jimmy called. "I'm here, I've got you."

He propelled himself forward and got hold of Hopper from behind, putting his arm round Hopper's chest so as to pull him on to his back. Then it would be easy for him to breathe as he was pulled along. But Hopper struggled like a person in a nightmare. He tried to beat Jimmy off as if Jimmy were an octopus.

Jimmy tried to call out to Hopper, to calm him, but they were fighting too fiercely. If he opened his mouth, water poured into it. So he concentrated on pulling Hopper over on to his back and kicking out for the shore. He would succeed in doing this for a few minutes, and then Hopper would struggle so violently that they would get twisted into a knot and start to sink. After one of these struggles, Jimmy managed to get Hopper into the right position and begin to move him along, but after a while he sensed that there was something wrong, and lifting his head he saw that they were going the wrong way and had moved some distance further out to sea. He tried to swing Hopper round in the water, but Hopper resisted again and began to thrash wildly with his arms.

"Drowning," he said.

"I've got you," Jimmy spluttered.

Hopper went down again. Jimmy pulled him up at the cost of going under himself. When he surfaced, their faces were close together and Hopper was looking straight into his eyes. But Jimmy could not tell whether Hopper recognised him or not.

"Help me," Hopper groaned, right into Jimmy's face.

"I've got you."

They struggled and swayed in the water. Then Hopper seemed to get cramp or something. He doubled up and his head went right under again Jimmy pulled him out and started to kick back towards the shore. Thank goodness, Hopper was quiet now. He had him in the correct grip and everything was going to be all right.

Jimmy was beginning to feel tired, but he did not slacken his efforts. There would be time to rest when they were on dry land. He kicked steadily, and held Hopper tight, and used his free arm in a backward crawl stroke. This went on for a long time, until Jimmy began to think that they must be getting in to shore. There must surely be other bathers round them. Perhaps he could call out and get a bit of help from someone. There would be nothing to be ashamed of in that, now he had brought Hopper out of danger. He lifted his head from the water, but could not see anyone close by. Still holding Hopper carefully out of the water, he twisted his body round to look towards the shore. It was no nearer. In fact the people walking about seemed like dots, and the bathing huts like dog kennels.

They were not getting any nearer to the shore. They must be in a current.

Jimmy kept calm. He had known these currents for years. This very one, he supposed, was the one he had planned to keep Hopper clear of. He had told Hopper exactly what part of the sea to go to, and Hopper had done as he said, but they were in the current all the same. That was because the currents were so unpredictable. They seemed to wander about the bay. This one was much further over than it usually came.

Hopper jerked up and down in the water. He got his face clear and gave a scream, up towards the clouds. It was as if he no longer cared about the land and had pinned all his hopes on being lifted up into the sky. He went under in mid-scream and it was obvious that his lungs had filled with water. Jimmy felt he ought to beat him on the back, but if he turned him face downwards to beat him on the back his face would be under water and his lungs would fill up faster than ever. Jimmy felt that stab of cold again. He had been afraid for some minutes, but this was different, this was panic. He wanted to shout for help himself.

Then a speckled gull came flapping slowly overhead, flying very low, examining the surface of the sea for traces of things to eat. It passed over Jimmy's head at a height of no more than three or four feet. At once Jimmy felt his panic leave him. The bird's presence seemed to domesticate the sea. Jimmy and Hopper were fighting for their lives, but to the gull this was just an ordinary afternoon and the sea was where it lives and where its food came from. The gull could at any time settle on the water and rest till it wanted to fly again. Well, so could a man.

Jimmy turned over on his back and floated, taking deep breaths and holding on to Hopper's arm: Hopper thrashed about a few more times, but Jimmy held on to his arm and let him get on with it. I'm the engine of this ship, he said to himself. If I rest a minute and get my strength back, I can get us out of this.

The water felt cold, and the strength took a long time to come back to Jimmy's muscles. But his brain was clear and he used the interval to think what to do. He knew from experience that the way to get clear of one of these currents was not to swim head-on against it, as he had been trying to do, but to swim diagonally through it, aiming at the shore but only indirectly, at an angle of thirty or forty degrees. When he felt able to start again, he steered at this angle, pulling Hopper with him. But at once he noticed a change in Hopper. He was not struggling, nor even holding his body rigid. He was simply floating on the water, offering no resistance. Jimmy lifted his head up and tried to look at Hopper's face, but it was difficult from that angle. Hopper seemed to have his eyes open: was that a good sign? Had he calmed down, trusting in Jimmy and waiting for them to get back to shallow water?

The current was dragging at them; Jimmy could feel it. He stopped thinking and put every atom of his strength into swimming steadily backwards at the angle he had chosen. His arms and legs worked like small, potent machines. Now and again, when fatigue threatened to put cramp into his muscles, he altered his stroke or varied the ratio of leg-thrusts to arm-thrusts. Hours seemed to go by. He did not dare raise himself and look towards the shore in case it was no nearer, or even further off. He knew that if it was he would despair and give up. But he must keep on, not only for his own sake but for Hopper's. He even thought, briefly, of Mr Prendergast and the Development Group, who had shown confidence in him.

Hopper would never forgive him. Ten pounds would not compensate him for a fright like this. He had passed out. Jimmy slammed shut the steel door of his mind against any other thought. Hopper had fainted, he was floating peacefully. He would soon come round when they got to shore. Jimmy understood about artificial respiration and the kiss of life. All he had to do was keep going, not faint himself. The only thing that could possibly make him faint was fear, the horrible suggestion that kept leaking out like gas through the steel doors. *Has he died? Are you swimming on and on without hope, towing a lump of dead meat through the water?*

And if he has died, wouldn't it be better to let the current carry you out to sea with him, both of you lost for ever, beyond recovery and beyond questioning?

Jimmy kept the steel doors shut and summoned up all the strength that remained to him. Soon he must either get to shore or be drowned. Suddenly, out of the corner of his eye, he saw a white, floating shape with a striped patch in the middle. It was the fat floating man whom he had passed on the way out, in what now seemed another life. He was lying on his back in the water as peacefully as Hopper. Jimmy reared up and looked round, letting Hopper float free for a moment. The shore was only about ten yards away, the Life Guard's hut was quite close, there were people playing and standing about in the water, he was there and nobody had noticed them struggling for their lives.

Jimmy was mistaken on this last point. In the usual patchy way in which things happen, some people had noticed that something was wrong and others had not. The fat man who was floating by himself was one of those who had not. But other people had seen Jimmy and Hopper and had called to one another and swum towards them. As Jimmy came in to the shore, they began to converge, and to call to friends on the beach, who came hurrying up. They gave instructions to each other and one tall man declared himself to be a doctor.

Jimmy bumped on the sand. They were safe. He stood up and found that the water came only to his knees. He bent over Hopper, who was floating like a wet log in the mild surf. Hopper's face was very stiff and his eyes were wide open. The salt water was washing in and out of his eyes: you would think he would have to shut them. Jimmy let go of Hopper and fell on to his hands and knees in the water and started vomiting.

Now he and Hopper were surrounded by a small crowd of people, wet swimmers and dry non-swimmers. They left Jimmy alone with his spreading patch of vomit that floated on the water, and pulled Hopper on to the sand. The doctor bent over him and everybody else stood by, jostling a little to see what was happening, but not talking much. Some children who were trying to see between the legs of the grown-ups were sent off to look for a policeman, partly because a policeman would be useful for taking statements and partly to stop them looking at Hopper.

Jimmy could hear nothing but his own retching, which was so loud that it seemed to fill the sky and press down on the sea. Between spasms he tried to tell God that he would do anything if only God would let Hopper not be dead. After a while he stopped retching and stood up. No one took any notice of him and he began to walk out of the water, past the stiff shape of Hopper and the bending and peering people. Then his way was blocked by the dark immovable bulk of the policeman.

Of course Jimmy knew the village policeman of Red Rocks, it was Mr Walker, there was nothing to be afraid of. But this was a new Mr Walker, slab-faced, hard, a taker of statements.

"I shall want your account of how this happened," he said.

"Is he – " said Jimmy. He could not say the word "dead".

"You were on duty and you saw that he was getting into difficulties?"

"I was in the sea. He called out," said Jimmy.

"Let the boy get dressed," said the doctor, looking up from where he knelt beside Hopper. "We don't want a pneumonia case on our hands as well as a death."

A death?

"Go and get dry and I'll take your statement in the hut," said policeman Walker to Jimmy.

They can't prove anything, said Jimmy inside himself

as he moved away. His legs were unsteady; his knees were very loose and everything else was very tight. He thought he would never stop shivering. They can't prove that Hopper did it because I offered to pay him. The current caught him, it might have happened to anybody. It was true what they said about the current. You could just manage it if you were on your own, a strong swimmer, but not with somebody else to hold up, it hadn't been his fault.

"I did my best," he said aloud. His voice was carried away down the beach by the unnoticing wind. "Nobody could have saved him," he said loudly. "He went too far out." Then he began to cry. Tears blurred the outline of the hut as he went towards it. Fumbling for the door handle, he got safely inside. A few people who came and stood near the hut could hear him sobbing.

"He's upset, poor lad."

"No wonder he's upset. He's supposed to stop this kind of thing happening, that's what he's there for."

Agnes, who was listening among the others, said nothing.

After about ten minutes, policeman Walker came up and rapped on the door of the hut.

"Are you ready to talk now, lad?" he called through the wood.

Jimmy opened the door. He was still not dressed or even dried.

"Come on, come on, lad," said the policeman not un-kindly. "Try not to go to pieces. You needn't give your evidence till later on if you don't feel up to it. Get along home and ask your mother to give you a cup of tea with a drop of whisky in it. I'll step up to the house later on."

"Is he –" Jimmy said again.

"They've done what they can for him," said the police-man. "But they haven't started him breathing and they never will now. His heart can't have been strong. There'll be a post mortem of course. If it does turn out that his heart was weak, that'll let you out of course."

"Let me out?"

"No dereliction of duty," said policeman Walker heavily.

"A man with a weak heart might die any time."

I didn't know he had a weak heart, God. He didn't even know it himself. He'd have said so, wouldn't he? Then I'd never have suggested the idea. Is God angry with me? Am I wicked, a murderer? Thou shalt not kill. Tell that to the sea, God. It was the sea killed him, sucked him under. *Help me*, he said. I'll see his face every night. *Help me*.

"I tried to," he said to the place where Hopper had stood. "I tried to help you."

"Get along home now," said policeman Walker.

As Jimmy walked up the long road between the straggling houses, he met two or three families walking the other way, towards the sea. They were carrying bathing costumes and towels and the children had buckets and spades. One child had a whizzer with celluloid wings that went round and round. These people had relaxed, holiday faces. They did not know that the afternoon had been darkened. They thought the sparkling waves were still innocent.

Jimmy's house was near the T-junction of the village. He had to walk the whole length of the road before he could go to his bedroom and be out of the sound of voices and the look of eyes. He would tell his mother he was exhausted from rescuing somebody and needed to rest. That would make her leave him alone, and later, when policeman Walker came to get his statement, he could pretend to be surprised that Hopper had died. He could say he thought the doctor was with him and that he would be all right. After all, though policeman Walker had said Hopper would never breathe again, he did not *know*. The doctor was still working on Hopper and perhaps it would all come right. Oh, God, make it come right.

Light footsteps pattered quickly after him. He turned, and it was Agnes who came running up. Jimmy stopped. There was a gap in the houses where they stood, and no one was near them.

"I s'pose you think you can just walk away," said Agnes. "Well, you can't. I know it was your fault Len got drowned."

Yes, that was Hopper's name, Len. At least that had been his name when he was alive.

"I tried to rescue him. The current's strong just there," said Jimmy.

"You killed him," said Agnes calmly.

"I –' he choked, "it was an accident."

"You gave him ten pounds to go swimming and get out of his depth."

"I never told him to get out of his depth."

"How could he pretend to be drowning if he wasn't? You killed him, Jimmy Townsend, it was you and nobody else."

"You can't prove it."

"I know where that piece of paper is. The one that says IOU."

"Why aren't you upset?" he asked her, suddenly curious about her calm blankness. "Don't you care about Hop – about Len?"

"I do care," she said. "I'm going to tell everybody that you killed him and then they'll hang you. Then that'll be fair."

"They won't hang me."

"They will when they know you killed him."

"They don't hang people any more."

"They'll lock you up in prison, Jimmy Townsend, for ever, and that's just as bad."

"It isn't," he said, thinking of the rope and the trap door.

"I'm going to take that piece of paper to Mr Walker."

"How d'you know about it, anyway?" he asked dully.

"I was listening through the door of the hut."

Little spy. She was as horrible as the most horrible side of Hopper. Jimmy glanced quickly to right and left, along the village street. There was no one about. He shot out his hand and grabbed Agnes's thin wrist. His fingers were very strong and he held the wrist in a fierce, pain-giving grip.

"Oh. Let me go. Let go of me."

"Listen," Jimmy breathed. "If you tell anybody what you heard, I'll kill you. I'll get at you and I'll kill you.

You say I killed Hopper, well, if I can be a murderer once I can be one twice."

"You're hurting me – you're breaking my –"

"They won't believe you anyway. It'll only be your word against mine because that paper doesn't say what the money was for and they can't prove anything. But I'll kill you just the same, I'll kill you, I'll kill you."

Without letting go of Agnes's wrist, he moved his other hand and gripped her by the shoulder. He had her backed against the churchyard wall now, holding her by the left wrist and right shoulder, hurting her in both places. Her bones felt as small and thin as a rabbit's. Suddenly it came to him that he was enjoying squeezing her in his hands. The strength of his fingers on Agnes's light bones was a pleasure to him because she was a girl. Even to hurt her was a pleasure. To hurt a boy would have been nothing.

At the thought, he took his hands off her as if she had become electrified, and stood back. She was crying, but calmly.

"That's something else you've done," she whispered. "Cruelty to children. I'm only ten."

Jimmy looked down at his hands. They seemed to him like the hands of a murderer. How had this happened to him? His nature had changed. All summer, till this, he had been as innocent as a seagull.

He stepped backward again, putting more space between himself and Agnes, as if to let her see that he was not going to attack her.

"Listen," he said. "I didn't mean it. I won't kill you. Tell them everything, see? I won't even be angry. I don't care any more. I shan't care when they take me away from here."

He could not explain, could not find words for his need to escape from his terrible, unrecognisable new self; and she said nothing. In the silence, Jimmy could hear the swish and boom of the waves on the beach. Turning his back on the sound, he walked rapidly away towards the village. Whatever happened, he knew that he would soon be leaving.

A & P

by John Updike

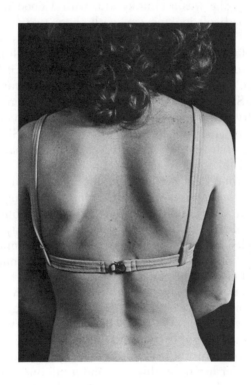

"A & P" is the name of an American supermarket chain, like Tesco. The initials stand for the "Great Atlantic and Pacific Tea Company". This branch is in the centre of a town some way from the sea. Sammy works at the checkout on the cash register. One day the ordinary workmanlike atmosphere is suddenly changed.

In walks these three girls in nothing but bathing suits. I'm in the second checkout slot, with my back to the door, so I don't see them until they're over by the bread. The one that caught my eye first was the one in the plaid green two-piece. She was a chunky kid, with a good tan and a sweet broad soft-looking can with those two crescents of white just under it, where the sun never seems to hit, at the top of the backs of her legs. I stood there with my hand on a box of HiHo crackers trying to remember if I rang it up or not. I ring it up again and the customer starts giving me hell. She's one of these cash-register-watchers, a witch about fifty with rouge on her cheekbones and no eyebrows, and I know it made her day to trip me up. She'd been watching cash registers for fifty years and probably never seen a mistake before.

By the time I got her feathers smoothed and her goodies into a bag – she gives me a little snort in passing, if she'd been born at the right time they would have burned her over in Salem – by the time I get her on her way the girls had circled around the bread and were coming back, without a pushcart, back my way along the counters, in the aisle between the checkouts and the Special bins. They didn't even have shoes on. There was this chunky one, with the two-piece – it was bright green and the seams on the bra were still sharp and her belly was still pretty pale so I guessed she just got it (the suit) – there was this one, with one of those chubby berry-faces, the lips all bunched together under her nose, this one, and a tall one, with black hair that hadn't quite frizzed right, and one of these sunburns right across under the eyes, and a chin that was too long – you know, the kind of girl other girls think is very "striking" and "attractive" but never quite makes it, as they very well know, which is why they like her so much – and then the third one, that wasn't quite so tall. She was the queen. She kind of led them, the other two peeking around and making their shoulders round. She didn't look around, not this queen, she just walked straight on slowly, on these long white prima-donna legs. She came down a little hard on her heels, as if she didn't walk in her bare feet that much, putting down her heels and then letting the weight move along to her toes as if she was testing the floor with every step, putting a little deliberate extra action into it. You never know for sure how girls' minds work (do you really think it's a mind in there or just a little buzz like a bee in a glass jar?) but you got the idea she had talked the other two into coming in here with her, and now she was showing them how to do it, walk slow and hold yourself straight.

She had on a kind of dirty-pink – beige maybe, I don't know – bathing suit with a little nubble all over it and, what got me, the straps were down. They were off her shoulders looped loose around the cool tops of her arms, and I guess as a result the suit had slipped a little on her, so all around the top of the cloth there was this shining rim. If it hadn't been there you wouldn't have known there could have been anything whiter than those shoulders. With the straps pushed off, there was nothing between the top of the suit and the top of her head except just *her*, this clean bare plane of the top of her chest down from the shoulder bones like a dented sheet of metal tilted in the light. I mean, it was more than pretty.

She had sort of oaky hair that the sun and salt had bleached, done up in a bun that was unravelling, and a kind of prim face. Walking into the A & P with your straps down, I suppose it's the only kind of face you *can* have. She held her head so high her neck, coming up out of those white shoulders, looked kind of stretched, but I didn't mind. The longer her neck was, the more of her there was.

She must have felt in the corner of her eye me and over my shoulder Stokesie in the first slot watching, but she didn't tip. Not this queen. She kept her eyes moving across the racks, and stopped, and turned so slow it made my stomach rub the inside of my apron, and buzzed to the other two, who kind of huddled against her for relief, and then they all three of them went up the cat-and-dog-food-breakfast-cereal-macaroni-rice-raisins-seasonings-spreads-spaghetti-soft-drinks-crackers-and-cookies aisle. From the second slot I look straight up the aisle to the meat counter,

31

and I watched them all the way. The fat one with the tan sort of fumbled with the cookies, but on second thought she put the package back. The sheep pushing their carts down the aisle – the girls were walking against the usual traffic (not that we have one-way signs or anything) – were pretty hilarious. You could see them, when Queenie's white shoulders dawned on them, kind of jerk, or hop, or hiccup, but their eyes snapped back to their own baskets and on they pushed. I bet you could set off dynamite in an A & P and the people would by and large keep reaching and checking oatmeal off their lists and muttering "Let me see, there was a third thing, began with A, asparagus, no, ah, yes, apple-sauce!" or whatever it is they do mutter. But there was no doubt, this jiggled them. A few house-slaves in pin curlers even looked around after pushing their carts past to make sure what they had seen was correct.

You know, it's one thing to have a girl in a bathing suit down on the beach, where what with the glare no-body can look at each other much anyway, and another thing in the cool of the A & P, under the fluorescent lights, against all those stacked packages, with her feet paddling along naked over our checkerboard green-and-cream rubber-tile floor.

"Oh Daddy," Stokesie said beside me. "I feel so faint."

"Darling," I said. "Hold me tight." Stokesie's married, with two babies chalked up on his fuselage already, but as far as I can tell that's the only difference. He's twenty-two, and I was nineteen this April.

"Is it done?" he asks, the responsible married man finding his voice. I forgot to say he thinks he's going to be manager some sunny day, maybe in 1990 when it's called the Great Alexandrov and Petrooshki Tea Company or something.

What he meant was, our town is five miles from a beach, with a big summer colony out on the Point, but we're right in the middle of town, and the women generally put on a shirt or shorts or something before they get out of the car into the street. And anyway these are usually women with six children and varicose veins mapping their legs and nobody, including them, could care less. As I say, we're right in the middle of town, and if you stand at our front doors you can see two banks and the Congregational church and the newspaper store and three real estate offices and about twenty-seven old freeloaders tearing up Central Street because the sewer broke again. It's not as if we're on the Cape; we're north of Boston and there's people in this town haven't seen the ocean for twenty years.

The girls had reached the meat counter and were asking McMahon something. He pointed, they pointed, and they shuffled out of sight behind a pyramid of Diet Delight peaches. All that was left for us to see was old McMahon patting his mouth and looking after them sizing up their joints. Poor kids, I began to feel sorry for them, they couldn't help it.

Now here comes the sad part of the story, at least my family says it's sad, but I don't think it's so sad myself. The store's pretty empty, it being Thursday afternoon, so there was nothing much to do except lean on the register and wait for the girls to show up again. The whole store was like a pinball machine and I didn't know which tunnel they'd come out of. After a while they come around out of the far aisle, around the light bulbs, records at discount of the Caribbean Six or Tony Martin Sings or some such junk you wonder they waste the wax on, six packs of candy bars, and plastic toys done up in cellophane that fall apart when a kid looks at them anyway. Around they come, Queenie still leading the way, and holding a little grey jar in her hand. Slots Three through Seven are unmanned and I could see her wondering between Stokes and me, but Stokesie with his usual luck draws an old party in baggy grey pants who stumbles up with four giant cans of pineapple juice (what do these bums *do* with all that pineapple juice? I've often asked myself) so the girls come to me. Queenie puts down the jar and I take it into my fingers icy cold. Kingfish Fancy Herring Snacks in Pure Sour Cream: 49c. Now her hands are empty, not a ring or a bracelet, bare as God made them, and I wonder where the money's coming from. Still with that prim look she lifts a folded dollar bill out of the hollow at the centre of her nubbled pink top. The jar went heavy in my hand. Really, I thought that was so cute.

Then everybody's luck begins to run out. Lengel comes in from haggling with a truck full of cabbages on the lot and is about to scuttle into that door marked MANAGER behind which he hides all day when the girls touch his eye. Lengel's pretty dreary, teaches Sunday school and the rest, but he doesn't miss that much. He comes over and says, "Girls, this isn't the beach."

Queenie blushes, though maybe it's just a brush of sunburn I was noticing for the first time, now that she was so close. "My mother asked me to pick up a jar of herring snacks." Her voice kind of startled me, the way voices do when you see the people first, coming out so flat and dumb yet kind of tony, too, the way it ticked over "pick up" and "snacks". All of a sudden I slid right down her voice into her living room. Her father and the other men were standing around in ice-cream coats and bow ties and the women were in sandals picking up herring snacks on toothpicks off a big glass plate and they were all holding drinks the colour of water with olives and sprigs of mint in them. When my parents have somebody over they get lemonade and if it's a real racy affair Schlitz in tall glasses with "They'll Do It Every Time" cartoons stencilled on.

"That's all right," Lengel said. "But this isn't the beach." His repeating this struck me as funny, as if it had just occurred to him, and he had been thinking all these years the A & P was a great big dune and he was the head lifeguard. He didn't like smiling—as I say he doesn't miss much—but he concentrates on giving the girls that sad Sunday-school-superintendent stare.

Queenie's blush is no sunburn now, and the plump one in plaid, that I liked better from the back—a really sweet can—pipes up. "We weren't doing any shopping. We just came in for the one thing."

"That makes no difference," Lengel tells her, and I could see from the way his eyes went that he hadn't noticed she was wearing a two-piece before. "We want you decently dressed when you come in here."

"We *are* decent," Queenie says suddenly, her lower lip pushing, getting sore now that she remembers her place, a place from which the crowd that runs the A & P must look pretty crummy. Fancy Herring Snacks flashed in her very blue eyes.

"Girls, I don't want to argue with you. After this come in here with your shoulders covered. It's our policy." He turns his back. That's policy for you. Policy is what the kingpins want. What the others want is juvenile delinquency.

All this while, the customers had been showing up with their carts but, you know, sheep, seeing a scene, they had all bunched up on Stokesie, who shook open a paper bag as gently as peeling a peach, not wanting to miss a word. I could feel in the silence everybody getting nervous, most of all Lengel, who asks me, "Sammy, have you rung up their purchase?"

I thought and said "No" but it wasn't about that I was thinking. I go through the punches, 4, 9, GROC, TOT—it's more complicated than you think, and after you do it often enough, it begins to make a little song, that you hear words to, in my case "Hello *(bing)* there, you *(gung)* hap-py *pee*-pul *(splat)*!"—the *splat* being the drawer flying out. I uncrease the bill, tenderly as you may imagine, it just having come from between the two smoothest scoops of vanilla I had ever known were there, and pass a half and a penny into her narrow pink palm, and nestle the herrings in a bag and twist its neck and hand it over, all the time thinking.

The girls, and who'd blame them, are in a hurry to get out, so I say "I quit" to Lengel quick enough for them to hear, hoping they'll stop and watch me, their unsuspected hero. They keep right on going, into the electric eye; the door flies open and they flicker across the lot to their car, Queenie and Plaid and Big Tall Goony-Goony (not that as raw material she was so bad), leaving me with Lengel and a kink in his eyebrow.

"Did you say something, Sammy?"

"I said I quit."

"I thought you did."

"You didn't have to embarrass them."

"It was they who were embarrassing us."

I started to say something that came out "Fiddle-de-doo". It's a saying of my grandmother's, and I know she would have been pleased.

"I don't think you know what you're saying," Lengel said.

"I know you don't," I said. "But I do." I pull the bow at the back of my apron and start shrugging it off my shoulders. A couple of customers that had been heading for my slot begin to knock against each other, like scared pigs in a chute.

Lengel sighs and begins to look very patient and old and grey. He's been a friend of my parents for years. "Sammy, you don't want to do this to your Mom and Dad," he tells me. It's true, I don't. But it seems to me that once you begin a gesture it's fatal not to go through with it. I fold the apron, "Sammy" stitched in red on the pocket, and put it on the counter, and drop the bow tie on top of it. The bow tie is theirs, if you've ever wondered. "You'll feel this for the rest of your life," Lengel says, and I know that's true, too, but remembering how he made that pretty girl blush makes me so scrunchy inside I punch the No Sale tab and the machine whirs "pee-pul" and the drawer splats out. One advantage to this scene taking place in summer, I can follow this up with a clean exit, there's no fumbling around getting your coat and galoshes, I just saunter into the electric eye in my white shirt that my mother ironed the night before, and the door heaves itself open, and outside the sunshine is skating around on the asphalt.

I look around for my girls, but they're gone, of course. There wasn't anybody but some young married screaming with her children about some candy they didn't get by the door of a powder-blue Falcon station wagon. Looking back in the big windows, over the bags of peat moss and aluminium lawn furniture stacked on the pavement, I could see Lengel in my place in the slot, checking the sheep through. His face was dark grey and his back stiff, as if he'd just had an injection of iron, and my stomach kind of fell as I felt how hard the world was going to be to me hereafter.

A Woman on a Roof

by Doris Lessing

Three men repairing a roof on a very hot day see a woman sunbathing. The sight affects them all in different ways. One of them, Tom, is only seventeen; he finds himself very disturbed. He plans a meeting.

It was during the week of hot sun, that June.

Three men were at work on the roof, where the leads got so hot, they had the idea of throwing water on to cool them. But the water steamed, then sizzled; and they made jokes about getting an egg from some woman in the flats under them, to poach it for their dinner. By two it was not possible to touch the guttering they were replacing, and they speculated about what workmen did in regularly hot countries. Perhaps they should borrow kitchen gloves with the egg? They were all a bit dizzy, not used to the heat; and they shed their coats and stood side by side squeezing themselves into a foot-wide patch of shade against a chimney, careful to keep their feet in the thick socks and boots out of the sun. There was a fine view across several acres of roofs. Not far off a man sat in a deck-chair reading the newspapers. Then they saw her, between chimneys, about fifty yards away. She lay face down on a brown blanket. They could see the top part of her: black hair, a flushed solid back, arms spread out.

"She's stark naked," said Stanley, sounding annoyed.

Harry, the oldest, a man of about forty-five, said: "Looks like it."

Young Tom, seventeen, said nothing, but he was excited and grinning.

Stanley said: "Someone'll report her if she doesn't watch out."

"She thinks no one can see," said Tom, craning his head all ways, to see more.

At this point the woman, still lying prone, brought her two hands up behind her shoulders with the ends of a scarf in them, tied it behind her back, and sat up. She wore a red scarf tied around her breasts and brief red bikini pants. This being the first day of the sun she was white, flushing red. She sat smoking, and did not look up when Stanley let out a wolf-whistle. Harry said: "Small things amuse small minds," leading the way back to their part of the roof, but it was scorching. Harry said: 'Wait, I'm going to rig up some shade,' and disappeared down the skylight into the building. Now that he'd gone, Stanley and Tom went to the farthest point they could to peer at the woman. She had moved, and all they would see were two pink legs stretched on the blanket. They whistled and shouted but the legs did not move. Harry came back with a blanket and shouted: "Come on, then." He sounded irritated with them. They clambered back to him and he said to Stanley: "What about your missus?" Stanley was newly married, about three months. Stanley said, jeering: "What about my missus?" – preserving his independence. Tom said nothing, but his mind was full of the nearly naked woman. Harry slung the blanket, which he had borrowed from a friendly woman downstairs, from the stem of a television aerial to a row of chimney pots. This shade fell across the piece of gutter they had to replace. But the shade kept moving, they had to adjust the blanket, and not much progress was made. At last some of the heat left the roof, and they worked fast, making up for lost time. First Stanley, then Tom, made a trip to the end of the roof to see the woman. "She's on her back," Stanley said, adding a jest which made Tom snicker, and the older man smile tolerantly. Tom's report was that she hadn't moved, but it was a lie. He wanted to keep what had seen to himself: he had caught her in the act of rolling down the little red pants over her hips till they were no more than a small triangle. She was on her back, fully visible, glistening with oil.

Next morning, as soon as they came up, they went to look. She was already there, face down, arms spread out, naked except for the little red pants. She had turned brown in the night. Yesterday she was a scarlet and white woman, today she was a brown woman. Stanley let out a whistle. She lifted her head, startled, as if she'd been asleep, and looked straight over at them. The sun was in her eyes, she blinked and stared, then she dropped her head again. At this gesture of indifference, they all three, Stanley, Tom and old Harry, let out whistles and yells. Harry was doing it in parody of the younger men, making fun of them, but he was also angry. They were all angry because of her utter indifference to the three men watching her.

"Bitch," said Stanley.

"She should ask us over," said Tom, snickering.

Harry recovered himself and reminded Stanley: "If she's married, her old man wouldn't like that."

"Christ," said Stanley virtuously, "if my wife lay about like that, for everyone to see, I'd soon stop her.'

Harry said, smiling: 'How do you know, perhaps she's sunning herself at this very moment?"

"Not a chance, not on our roof." The safety of his wife put Stanley into a good humour, and they went to work. But today it was hotter than yesterday; and several times one or the other suggested they should tell Matthew, the foreman, and ask to leave the roof until the heat-wave was over. But they didn't There was work to be done in the basement of the big block of flats, but up here they felt free, on a different level from ordinary humanity shut in the streets or the buildings. A lot more people came out on to the roofs that day, for an hour at midday. Some married couples sat side by side in deck-chairs, the women's legs stockingless and scarlet, the men in vests with reddening shoulders.

The woman stayed on her blanket, turning herself over and over. She ignored them, no matter what they did. When Harry went off to fetch more screws, Stanley said: "Come on." Her roof belonged to a different system of roofs, separated from theirs at one point by about twenty feet. It meant a scrambling climb from one level to another, edging along parapets, clinging to chimneys, while their big boots slipped and slithered, but at last they stood on a small square projecting roof looking straight down at her, close. She sat smoking, reading a book. Tom thought she looked like a poster, or a magazine cover, with the blue sky behind her and her legs stretched out. Behind her a great crane at work on a new building in Oxford Street swung its black arm across the roofs in a great arc. Tom imagined himself at work on the crane, adjusting the arm to swing over and pick her up and swing her back across the sky to drop her near him.

They whistled. She looked up at them, cool and remote, then went on reading. Again, they were furious. Or rather, Stanley was. His sun-heated face was screwed into rage as he whistled again and again, trying to make her look up. Young Tom stopped whistling. He stood beside Stanley excited, grinning; but he felt as if he were saying to the woman: "Don't associate me with *him*," for his grin was apologetic. Last night he had thought of the unknown woman before he slept, and she had been tender with him. This tenderness he was remembering as he shifted his feet by the jeering, whistling Stanley, and watched the indifferent, healthy brown woman a few feet off, with the gap that plunged to the street between them. Tom thought it was romantic, it was like being high on two hill-tops. But there was a shout from Harry, and they clambered back. Stanley's face was hard, really angry. The boy kept looking at him and wondered why he hated the woman so much, for already he loved her.

They played their little games with the blanket, trying to trap shade to work under; but again it was not until nearly four that they could work seriously, and they were exhausted, all three of them. They were grumbling about the weather, by now. Stanley was in a thoroughly bad humour. When they made their routine trip to see the woman before they packed up for the day, she was apparently asleep, face down, her back all naked save for the scarlet triangle on her buttocks. "I've got a good mind to report her to the police," said Stanley, and Harry said: "What's eating you? What harm's she doing?"

"I tell you, if she was my wife!"

"But she isn't, is she?" Tom knew that Harry, like himself, was uneasy at Stanley's reaction. He was normally a sharp young man, quick at his work, making a lot of jokes, good company.

"Perhaps it will be cooler tomorrow?" said Harry.

But it wasn't, it was hotter, if anything, and the weather forecast said the good weather would last. As soon as they were on the roof, Harry went over to see if the woman were there, and Tom knew it was to prevent Stanley going, to put off his bad humour. Harry had grown-up children, a boy the same age as Tom, and the youth trusted and looked up to him.

Harry came back and said: "She's not there."

"I bet her old man has put his foot down," said Stanley, and Harry and Tom caught each other's eyes and smiled behind the young married man's back.

Harry suggested they should get permission to work in the basement, and they did, that day. But before packing up Stanley said: "Let's have a breath of fresh air." Again Harry and Tom smiled at each other as they followed Stanley up to the roof, Tom in the devout conviction that he was there to protect the woman from Stanley. It was about five-thirty, and a calm full sunlight lay over the roofs. The great crane still swung its black arm from Oxford Streets to above their heads. She was not there. Then there was a flutter of white from behind a parapet, and she stood up, in a belted white dressing-gown. She had been there all day, probably, but on a different patch of roof, to hide from them. Stanley did not whistle, he said nothing, but watched the woman bend to collect papers, books, cigarettes, then fold the blanket over her arm. Tom was thinking: If they weren't here, If they weren't here, I'd go over and say...What? But he knew from his nightly dreams of her that she was kind and friendly. Perhaps she would ask him down in to her flat? Perhaps...he stood watching her disappear down the skylight. As she went, Stanley let out a shrill derisive yell, she started, and it seemed as if she nearly fell. She clutched to save herself, they could hear things falling. She looked straight at them, angry. Harry said, facetiously: "Better be careful on those slippery ladders, love." Tom knew he said it to save her from Stanley, but she could not know it. She vanished, frowning. Tom was full of a secret delight, because he knew her anger was for the others, not for him.

"Roll on some rain," said Stanley, bitter, looking at the blue evening sky.

Next day was cloudless, and they decided to finish the work in the basement. They felt excluded, shut in the grey cement basement fitting pipes, from the holiday atmosphere of London in a heat-wave. At lunchtime they came up for some air, but while the married couples, and the men in shirt-sleeves or vests, were there, she was not there, either on her usual patch of roof or where she had been yesterday. They all, even Harry, clambered about, between chimney-pots, over parapets, the hot leads stinging their fingers. There was not a sign of her. They took off their shirts and vests and exposed their chests, feeling their feet sweaty and hot. They did not mention the woman. But Tom felt alone again. Last night she had asked him into her flat: it was big and had fitted white carpets and a bed with a padded white leather head-top. She wore a black filmy négligé and her kindness to Tom thickened his throat as he remembered it. He felt she had betrayed him by not being there.

And again after work they climbed up, but still there was nothing to be seen of her. Stanley kept repeating that if it was as hot as this tomorrow he wasn't going to work and that's all there was to it. But they were all there next day. By ten the temperature was in the middle seventies, and it was eighty long before noon. Harry went to the foreman to say it was impossible to work on the leads in that heat; but foreman said there was nothing else he could put them on, and they'd have to. At midday they stood, silent, watching the skylight on her roof open, and then she slowly emerged in her white gown, holding a bundle of blankets. She looked at them, gravely, then went to the part of the roof where she was hidden from them. Tom was pleased. He felt she was more his when the other men couldn't see her. They had taken off their shirts and vests, but now they put them back again, for they felt the sun bruising their flesh. "She must have the hide of a rhino," said Stanley, tugging at guttering and swearing. They stopped work, and sat in the shade, moving around behind chimney stacks. A wo-man came to water a yellow window-box just opposite them. She was middleaged, wearing a flowered summer dress. Stanley said to her: "We need a drink more than them." She smiled and said: "Better drop down to the pub quick, it'll be closing in a minute." They exchanged pleasantries, and she left them with a smile and a wave.

"Not like Lady Godiva," said Stanley. "She can give us a bit of a chat and a smile."

"You don't whistle at *her*," said Tom, reproving.

"Listen to him," said Stanley, "you didn't whistle then?"

But the boy felt as if he hadn't whistled, as if only Tom and Stanley had. He was making plans, when it was time to knock off work, to get left behind and somehow make his way over to the woman. The weather report said the hot spell was due to break, so he had to move quickly. But there was no chance of being left. The other two decided to knock off work at four, because they were exhausted. As they went down, Tom quickly climbed a parapet and hoisted himself higher by pulling his weight up a chimney. He caught a glimpse of her lying on her back, her knees up, eyes closed, a brown woman lolling in the sun. He slipped and clattered down, as Stanley looked for information: "She's gone down," he said. He felt as if he had protected her from Stanley, and that she must be grateful to him. He could feel the bond between the woman and himself.

Next day, they stood around on the landing below the roof, reluctant to climb up into the heat. The woman who had lent Harry the blanket came out and offered them a cup of tea. They accepted gratefully, and sat around Mrs Pritchett's kitchen an hour or so, chatting. She was married to an airline pilot. A smart blonde, of about thirty, she had an eye for the handsome sharpfaced Stanley; and the two teased each other while Harry sat in a corner, watching, indulgent, though his expression reminded Stanley that he was married. And young Tom felt envious of Stanley's ease in badinage; felt, too, that Stanley's getting off with Mrs Pritchett left his romance with the woman on the roof safe and intact.

"I thought they said the heat-wave'd break," said Stanley, sullen, as the time approached when they really would have to climb up into the sunlight.

"You don't like it, then?" asked Mrs Pritchett.

"All right for some," said Stanley. "Nothing to do but lie about as if it was a beach up there. Do you ever go up?"

"Went up once," said Mrs Pritchett. "But it's a dirty place up there, and it's too hot."

"Quite right too," said Stanley.

Then they went up, leaving the cool neat little flat and the friendly Mrs Pritchett.

As soon as they were up they saw her. The three men looked at her, resentful at her ease in this punishing sun. Then Harry said, because of the expression on Stanley's face: "Come on, we've got to pretend to work, at least."

They had to wrench another length of guttering that ran beside a parapet out of its bed, so that they could replace it. Stanley took it in his two hands, tugged, swore, stood up. "F – it," he said, and sat down under a chimney. He lit a cigarette. "F – them," he said, "what do they think we are, lizards? I've got blisters all over my hands." Then he jumped up and climbed over the roofs and stood with his back to them. He put his fingers either side of his mouth and let out a shrill whistle. Tom and Harry squatted, not looking at each other, watching him. They could just see the woman's head, the beginnings of her brown shoulders. Stanley whistled again. Then he began stamping with his feet, and whistled and yelled and screamed at the woman, his face getting scarlet. He seemed quite mad, as he stamped and whistled, while the woman did not move, she did not move a muscle.

"Barmy," said Tom.

"Yes," said Harry, disapproving.

Suddenly the older man came to a decision. It was, Tom knew, to save some sort of scandal or real trouble over the woman. Harry stood up and began packing tools into a length of oily cloth. "Stanley," he said, commanding. At first Stanley took no notice, but Harry said: "Stanley, we're packing it in, I'll tell Matthew."

Stanley came back, cheeks mottled, eyes glaring.

"Can't go on like this," said Harry. "It'll break in a day or so. I'm going to tell Matthew we've got sunstroke, and if he doesn't like it, it's too bad." Even Harry sounded aggrieved, Tom noted. The small, competent man, the family man with his grey hair, who was never at a loss, sounded really off balance. "Come on," he said, angry. He fitted himself into the open square in the roof, and went down, watching his feet on the ladder. Then Stanley went, with not a glance at the woman. Then Tom who, his throat beating with excitement, silently promised her in a backward glance: Wait for me, wait, I'm coming.

On the pavement Stanley said: "I'm going home." He looked white now, so perhaps he really did have sunstroke. Harry went off to find the foreman who was at work on the plumbing of some flats down the street. Tom slipped back, not into the building they had been working on, but the building on whose roof the woman lay. He went straight up, no one stopping him. The skylight stood open, with an iron ladder leading up. He emerged on to the roof a couple of yards from her. She sat up, pushing back her black hair with both hands. The scarf across her breasts bound them tight, and brown flesh bulged around it. Her legs were brown and smooth. She stared at him in silence. The boy stood grinning, foolish, claiming the tenderness he expected from her.

"What do you want?" she asked.

"I . . . I came to . . . make your acquaintance," he stammered, grinning, pleading with her.

They looked at each other, the slight, scarlet-faced excited boy, and the serious, nearly-naked woman. Then, without a word, she lay face down on her brown blanket, ignoring him.

"You like the sun, do you?" he inquired of her glistening back.

Nor a word. He felt panic, thinking of how she had held him in her arms, stroked his hair, brought him where he sat, lordly, in her bed, a glass of some exhilarating liquor he had never tasted in life. He felt that if he knelt down, stroked her shoulders, her hair, she would turn and clasp him in her arms.

He said: "The sun's all right for you, isn't it."

She raised her head, set her chin on two small fists. "Go away," she said. He did not move. "Listen," she said, in a slow reasonable voice, where anger was kept in check, though with difficulty; looking at him, her face weary with anger: "If you get a kick out of seeing women in

46

bikinis, why don't you take a sixpenny bus ride to the Lido? You'd see dozens of them, without all this mountaineering."

She hadn't understood him. He felt her unfairness pale him. He stammered: "But I like you, I've been watching you and . . ."

"Thanks," she said, and dropped her face again, turned away from him.

She lay there. He stood there. She said nothing. She had simply shut him out. He stood, saying nothing at all, for some minutes. He thought: She'll have to say something if I stay. But the minutes went past, with no sign of them in her, except in the tension of her back, her thighs, her arms, – the tension of waiting for him to go.

He looked up at the sky, where the sun seemed to spin in heat; and over the roofs where he and his mates had been earlier. He could see the heat quivering where they had worked. And they expect us to work in these conditions! he thought, filled with righteous indignation. The woman hadn't moved. A bit of hot wind blew her black hair softly, it shone, and was iridescent. He remembered how he had stroked it last night.

Resentment of her at last moved him off and away down the ladder, through the building, into the street. He got drunk then, in hatred of her.

Next day when he woke the sky was grey. He looked at the wet and thought, viciously: Well that's fixed you, hasn't it now? That's fixed you good and proper.

The three men were at work early on the cool leads, surrounded by damp drizzling roofs where no one came to sun themselves, black roofs, slimy with rain. Because it was cool now, they would finish the job that day, if they hurried.

First Kiss

by Philip Callow

*A young man is making a determined effort to kiss hi.
first girl. Will he succeed? Is he really interested in he*

Sitting in the coach, going to meet her, I had decided. And long before that. I would kiss a woman tonight, for the first time. Yes; she would be the one. I intended to kiss her full on the mouth.

To be twenty-five, a grown man, and not to have kissed a woman, was serious. The problem only became more tormenting if I brought it up to the light and tried to consider it. It was a thing to be kept hidden. Even when I was an apprentice and under twenty-one, workmates of my age were always messing about with girls at night, "necking" in front rooms and at cinemas. Was there something wrong with me? No one regarded me as a ninny, yet how could I call myself a man without this knowledge? The leper feeling and the longing to indulge my senses were both very real.

Now I had my chance, and not with a mere girl. With a ripe woman. The coach rushed me on, full of purpose, momentous, across the flat Midlands country. I sank back in the springs and stared out in the ashy light, at the stagnant autumn fields. Yet nothing looked hopeless or dreary, as it usually did. It all seemed hushed and grave and atmospheric, in the dead afternoon. There was no sun. Slowly the dusk thickened round us like brown fog, settling between the hedges and drifting in among the rain-backened trees. We sped along in fairly open country for a few more miles. I must have been day-dreaming, because when I looked out again we were gliding through damp, narrowing tunnels of streets.

At the terminus I stepped out stiffly into the market square. When I moved away from the lighted windows of the coach, it was pitch dark. I began to pick my way carefully to the edge of this large black space, towards some bright splashes and blots of light.

I found a cheap café. It would do for the few minutes I had to wait. I took my cup of tea from the counter and went hesitating amongst all the blank tables and chairs. I wondered vaguely where everyone could be on a Saturday night.

A man came in with a thick bundle of Michaelmas

daisies that had been battered by the rain. The stems were lashed together like sticks, with some hairy white string. He ignored all the other vacant places and sat on the next chair to me, undoing his greasy overcoat fastidiously, using one hand. I waited for him to speak or go over to the counter. He gave me sideways glances, sizing me up.

"Bitter wind," he rasped suddenly, twisting his head.

"Bitter," I said.

I sipped my hot tea. The man at my side was rustling his daisies, and I thought he was putting them down somewhere. Without warning his arm shot out and he brandished a separate bunch of flowers level with my eyes.

"Tanner," he stated. He turned them round.

"No, thanks."

"How much?"

I shook my head.

"I'm a stranger," I said meaninglessly.

He lurched to his feet and blundered out without another word.

At last it was time. I left the café and strode up to the deserted corner, repressed, and Claire jumped out of a shop doorway.

"Ha ha," she said, radiant, standing in front of me and smiling. "Didn't you see me?"

I shook my head. It was always the same; I had a struggle to get anything out for the first few minutes. Then it got better.

"I was keeping out of the wind, it's like a knife on this corner," she blurted out nervously.

We were shy of one another. At the bus-stop she took my arm very quietly, and I kept my head turned away looking for the bus we wanted, as if nothing had happened.

"Come on, bus – quick, quick," I groaned in mock anguish. In two hours she would be gone.

"Aren't you in a hurry!" she laughed, pleased with the flattery. Already she had recovered her poise.

The early November wind blew in gusts against us, wintry. We both shivered and hugged ourselves in, standing together politely.

"Cold?" I asked.

She nodded, shuddering her shoulders extravagantly.

"You'll have to warm me up," she whispered gaily. I felt suddenly joyous and grateful. She was encouraging me. I would be able to kiss her and be initiated. It was almost accomplished.

The bus lumbered into sight and drew up for us alone, as if we had ordered it. Claire stepped on, erect and springy, and I clambered in after her, very tense.

"What do I ask for?" I said hurriedly, with the burly conductor swaying over us.

"North Bridge," she told me.

There was a walk she knew by the river. We had decided to go there.

The trolley-bus trundled forward for a short distance and slowed down, creaking. I did not realise it was electric at first. I heard the hissing for the first time as it shunted away again, jerking and gathering speed, like a train.

It was warm inside. We sat without making any sign, our sides touching. Claire was at the window. I tried to become calmer, and get control of myself, but the opposite seemed to be happening. The great favour I felt bestowed on me by this woman who sat pressed warmly against my hip and shoulder, the lovely contact, the thought of her long thighs, of us drawing steadily nearer to the waiting place of darkness, and the kiss, all began to overwhelm me. Under my overcoat I was quivering. I fought to stop it.

Claire noticed the vibration, feeling it on her shoulder.

"Still cold?" she asked, turning to me and smiling brilliantly.

"Yes, a bit," I said, gripping myself hard.

"You're nesh, like me."

"I'm what?" I was familiar with the word, but we never used it in my part of the Midlands.

"Nesh – always cold." She laughed in my face, gay and reckless. "Don't you know it?"

"I've heard it before; I wasn't sure what it meant," I said solemnly.

"What do *you* call it, then?" She gave her quick laugh again.

"Starved," I said.

She was not listening any longer. She peered out to see if we were there.

"Another stop," she announced, almost triumphant.

"I'm lost," I grinned. It pleased me to say it aloud because it emphasised the strangeness. I wanted Claire to be aware of this too.

We started to get off. Claire stalked ahead of me, jumped down to the wide pavement and twirled round, her dark eyes flaring. As a girl she must have appeared haughty and unapproachable, I thought, but now she was full of bold invitation. Her sensitive girl's mouth had been overcome by something else, perhaps irony. She was bitterly ironic about herself.

She had a long, quiet stride that was almost stealthy, cat-like. She kept up with me easily. We left the road and began to descend a concrete ramp between shrubs with large glossy leaves. Suddenly an urge rose up in me to appear impulsive, to answer the challenge of the looks she kept giving me, and at the same time I saw a way of taking hold of her hand. I was afraid of making it too significant.

"Run!" I cried, grabbing her hand violently and pulling her forward.

It was a success. We arrived breathless and laughing at the bottom, where a gas-lamp fixed high up on a bracket shone on two wooden posts set in the cement. The polished branches of a gas-lit tree jutted out, looking exposed and sinister. Dead leaves were blowing from the tops of the loose heaps, turning over and scratching on the hard path.

Claire still held firmly to my hand, so I tightened my grip. We walked forward on either side of the high middle post, and instead of letting go she swung up her arm and mine quickly to make an arch, so that our hands cleared the top. It must have looked courtly, as if we were dancers in another century.

She gave my fingers a sudden squeeze to convey her pleasure. I was excited. I felt an extraordinary confidence. Everything I saw was personal and had a tender glow around it. The lights of cars and buses slipped by above the parapet of the bridge we had just left. They gave off a soft humming sound.

There seemed to be a hedge now on our left, and to the right it was all open. The river was that side. We drew near to another lamp.

"Look, some Old Man's Beard," she said.

"Where?"

"There, look." She pointed up at the hedge, to some bits of greyish fluff.

"Is that what it's called?"

"Well, it's really clematis."

"Oh,"

"Aren't I knowledgeable!" she said, giggling.

"Very," I said. I knew nothing about flowers and plants.

I laughed shakily, proud of my ignorance, of my difference to her in all kinds of ways. I sensed that she appreciated me because I was not dipped in her sort of experiences. There was no patronage: I was being deliciously flattered. And the knowledge in her subtly smiling eyes made her weaker, though bolder than me. I was all expectation, trembling and strong. Nothing divided me, I did not know enough. She guessed my purity and drew closer, wanting to taste me.

The river path was ordinary earth. It squelched under our feet. There were no more lamps now; we had just gone by the last one. The water was invisible, moving noiselessly, but it seemed to give off a faint light. Then some dense bushes reared up and blotted even that out. Darkness closed round us like a bag. I moved my legs deliberately, forcing them – they were sightless and wanted to stop.

"It's drier over here," Claire hissed, tugging and guiding me. She found it funny.

There was a small splash.

"What was that?" she asked sharply.

"My foot," I said. "Thanks very much."

"There you are, that's a lesson for you," she chuckled in great glee. "Never trust a woman."

"No," I said.

We walked along. All at once she started, and shrank against me.

"I heard something move," she whispered, in a humble voice.

"Where?"

"In the hedge. Behind it."

"Nothing can hurt you," I said strongly. We had stopped.

"No, I know," came her voice, still small. "I can't understand why I was so frightened."

We went on again. She clung fast to my arm and I could feel myself taking manly, clumping steps. I was being protective and dependable. It amazed me to realise this, and still I did not feel foolish. It gave me great satisfaction.

At last we found a seat and sat at one end, huddled in our clothes, holding hands rather primly. Gradually my eyes made out her face. Then a blurred moon appeared and began to race distractedly across a gulf in the sky. The wind ebbed and flowed round our heads, dragging and pressing, sucking at our hair. There was a steady stream of coldness, even without the wind.

"We're mad," Claire said, and her voice sounded tender.

"Yes," I murmured. She was so near I kept coiling within myself, in apprehension. Did she want me to kiss her? The very thought of her large eyes unnerved me. I prayed for the moon to be swallowed up.

"I like to do mad things," she crooned.

Something in her voice thrilled me, and I took her words for encouragement. With a despairing, clumsy movement I twisted towards her. My heart was plunging about. Claire allowed her head to sink back, and she closed her eyes calmly. Her eyelids were bluish. They looked nerve-worn and pathetic, and I put my face down thankfully to cover her neat mouth that was pouting slightly. It was perfectly natural, my nose was not in the way, and I thought: "How easy it is!" Already I had forgotten the eyes shutting very quickly to help me, after seeing what a novice I was. I kissed her, dazed with relief, all my famished youth and unused tenderness going into the kiss and making it fierce.

The moon was covered up again. In the dark I touched the curious shapes of her chin and cheeks and short nose. The skin of her face was rough with frost, lying hard and frozen under my lips. I tasted the cold and it repelled me. She was hardly real. Gropingly I found her again where she was alive with warm breath, kissing her without passion until the lips softened and went slack, forming a lovely mouth.

It was a new world, a happiness. Her opened lips were incredibly soft. I had never experienced anything like it before. My sensuality broke free like a starved prisoner, to feed and gorge itself. It was wonderful to let it out gladly, instead of throttling it and being tormented afterwards.

She gripped me hard, in a sudden frenzy. Then she clung against me, not speaking, just nestling close and hugging my head to her. Desire bristled in me, but I pitied her too much, and the pain of existence was too close, mixing into the gladness. Her hand stroked my head. I thought how naive we were, comforting one another in this simple way, like children. But what other consolation was there? People were mad to insult it, to treat it with contempt. There was nothing else.

When our feet grew numb and painful and we stumbled up, gasping, I felt sharp with joy and pride. She had wanted me to kiss her. We walked along stiffly, laughing at each other.

Later we went back to stand under the arch of the bridge for a little while, partly out of the wind. The stone was wet. Claire slipped her arms inside my overcoat, around my corduroy jacket waist.

"Ah, you're wearing velvet," she whispered. "Nice."

I pressed my mouth to her throat, suddenly chilled by the thought of this sensuousness about to be taken away.

"I love your fire," she said very softly, into the draughty space of the arch.

Then she disengaged herself and began to harden her

face and voice, as if getting ready to enter the narrow struggling world of streets and buses and other people again. It was horrible, but I said nothing. I even hated her for being what she was, so easily changed by that world, readily adapting herself. I was far too exalted to be reasonable. I watched her powdering her face and thought how crude and ugly her gestures were. Before this night I would never have judged her. I was much closer, different now. I considered I had the right.

She sent me home, and went back with her kisses to her husband. I was confused, beaten and elated by everything. I did not stay bitter long.

Next day was Sunday. I lay in bed until nearly eleven; I had been awake for hours. The noise of the wind outside made me feel frail. It rumbled against the walls and went clattering among the sheds and fences and bits of loose tin, full of angry power. When I got up, people spoke to me and I only half heard them.

Then on Monday, as I stood at my bench in the factory, a youth I went about with sometimes in the evenings came up to me. I was glad to see him. I had been waiting for a chance to speak.

"What d'you know?" Harry said.

"Not much," I said, giving the stock answer.

His sleepy eyes looked at me.

"Go anywhere Saturday night?"

I nodded. "I went to meet a woman," I said mysteriously.

"Go on," he said, disbelieving and scornful.

He was already engaged, and so a trifle superior. As far as he knew, I didn't have anybody.

"In Warwick," I told him. At the last moment some instinct had made me give a false place.

"What was she like, then?" he asked curiously, but without any respect.

I looked back steadily.

"She can't get enough of me," I said.

And his eyes opened wide.

Ellen

by Morley Callaghan

Ellen is Mr Mason's only child. His wife has left him, and now his daughter has grown up. Will she be happy? It means a great deal to him.

Old Mr Mason had always longed with a desperate earnestness that his daughter, Ellen, should be happy, and now she was in trouble. She had lived alone with him ever since she had been a little girl. Years ago his wife, after a long time of bickering and secret bitterness over his failure to get along in business, had left him, left him to a long monotony of steady working days and evenings at home, listening to music from the gramophone or waiting for election time so that he could go to the meetings. He had hoped for a bright joyousness in Ellen's life, and whenever he heard her laugh, saw how independently she walked along the street, and felt her cool reticence, he was sure she would be content. Ellen was a small girl with little hands and feet, blue eyes set far apart, and a wide forehead and a face that tapered smoothly to her chin. She had never had much money, but she wore her clothes with such grace that, with her natural assurance, she looked almost elegant.

Before going out in the evenings, whenever she had a new hat or dress and was sure of her beauty, she used to pretend to annoy her father, who was reading his paper, by saying coaxingly, "Please tell me that I don't look a fright. Could anybody say I looked pretty, Dad?" And she would smile to herself with secret amusement while he was saying, "You're a beauty, Ellen, Bless my soul, if you're not! When I was a young fellow, I'd twist my neck out of place on the street if a girl like you passed by." Until she went out the front door he would wait, apparently interested only in his paper; then he would jump up and hurry to the window with his pipe in one hand and the paper under the other arm and watch her hurrying along the street with her short, rapid steps.

From the beginning she had been very much in love with Joe Eaton. Joe was a handsome, good-natured fellow – a big, broad-shouldered young man with a fine head of untidy brown hair who laughed often, was always at ease, and was marvellously gentle with Ellen when he was with her. This gentleness in such a big man used to make Mr Mason warm with joy, and sometimes when he went to bed after watching Joe and Ellen, it seemed wonderful that Ellen should have the love of a man who had so much tenderness for her. Joe Eaton hadn't much money but he wanted to be an architect and he loved the work, and he liked talking about the things he planned to do, especially when he and Ellen had come into the house with the elation of two children after the evening out together. Ellen used to listen to him with a grave wonder, and then, a little later, with laughter in her eyes, she would try to get him to tease her father. Joe could tell stories that would keep them all laughing till two o'clock in the morning, especially if he had brought a bottle or two of red wine. Three times Mr Mason coaxed Joe to play a game of checkers and then enjoyed giving him a bad beating; Joe was too impulsive to be a success at the game.

Mr Mason had hoped that Ellen and Joe would get married and have a place of their own, and after a year, perhaps, he hoped they might invite him to go and live with them. But instead of that, Joe stopped coming to the house. "He's gone. It's over. We won't see him again," Ellen said. Her solemn face could not conceal her fierce resentment.

She went from day to day with a set little smile on her face, and there was growing in her a strange gravity and stillness that made her father, watching her, ache with disappointment. They used to get up in the morning at the same hour and have breakfast together before going out to work. Her face on these mornings looked pinched and weary, as if she had not slept, and her blue eyes, which at first had shown so easily that she was hurt, now had a dull expression of despair. Yet she walked along the street in the old way, dressed smartly in bright colours, her body erect, and when she came home in the evenings and saw her father looking at her anxiously, she wrinkled the corners of her mouth into a smile and began, "Do you know, Dad, the most amusing thing happened today..." She would begin to tell some trivial story, but in a few moments she was so grave again that she frightened him.

Mr Mason began to get so upset that he hardly knew

what he was doing. One night he left Ellen sitting by herself in the living-room and went into his bedroom to read himself to sleep. He had put on his nightgown and standing on the carpet in his bare feet, staring at the reading light with his evening paper under his arm. The pillows were propped up on the bed, as they were every night, and he patted them with his hand. At last he sighed, half smiled, and dragged himself into bed as if his old body were heavy with disappointment. The reading light shone on his white head and on the intricate network of veins on his red neck as he lay back with his glasses in his hand. "There's no use worrying and wondering about these things," he said to himself, so he set his glasses firmly on his nose and started turning the pages of the paper. But no matter how he stared, or even rubbed his hand over his eyes, he kept on having the same thought. All of a sudden he sat up and felt a surge of anger. The hand holding the paper began to tremble, his face got as red with the sudden rush of blood at the back of his neck, and it looked as if he were going to have one of his rare bursts of bad temper. He felt a hatred of Joe Eaton, a resentment against all the days of the past year. "This has got to end," he thought. "Ellen's not going to worry herself and me into the grave. What's she doing sitting in that room by herself at this hour? I'll tell her to go to bed. I'll put an end to this once and for all."

He hurried, throwing his old brown dressing-gown around him, feeling strong with independence. With his old slippers slapping on the floor, and his white hair, ruffled by the pillow, sticking out from his head at all angles, he went striding along the hall to the living-room.

The light was out, but from the door he could see Ellen sitting over by the window with her elbows on the sill. First he coughed, then he walked over softly and sat down on a chair beside her. Moonlight was shining on the side of her face, touching her wide forehead where her long hair was pushed back from her temples. He suddenly wanted to touch her cheek and her hair, but he was determined to speak firmly. He did not know how to begin such a conversation. He said very hesitantly, "Aren't you up late, Ellen?"

"Weren't you able to sleep. Dad?" she said.

"Yes, but I didn't want you sitting in here feeling alone."

"It isn't late, and I'm all right."

"The house seemed so quiet," he said. "I got thinking you might be feeling lonely. I got thinking of Joe Eaton, too. Are you thinking he might still marry you?"

"He can't marry me. He's not here to marry me. He's gone away to Detroit." And, still without turning her head to look at him, she said, "It will get unpleasant for you, Dad. If you don't want me to stay here, I won't. Soon the neighbours will notice me and begin to talk."

He thought she must hear his heart beating with such slow heaviness that it hurt him, and he said, "I wasn't thinking anything like that."

"It doesn't take people long to notice things," she said.

"Ellen, it's all right. Don't waste yourself on such thoughts. I know you can't be happy, but try not to feel miserable," he said. His voice faltered, he thought he was going to lose control of himself. Then he said with simple dignity, "I'll look after you as long as I live, you know. Please don't feel miserable."

"I don't, Dad," she said, turning toward him. He saw the soft light on all her face. Her face was so smooth and serene that he was startled. There was a sweet, full contentment in it he had never seen before. The soft light gave her face a glowing happiness.

"Ellen," he whispered. "You look happy, child."

"I'm very happy," she said.

"Why are you so happy? How can you have such a feeling?"

"I feel very contented now, that's all," she said simply. "Tonight everything is so still on the street outside and in the dark here. I was so very happy while Joe was with me," she whispered. "It was as though I had never been alive before. It's so sweetly peaceful tonight, waiting, and feeling so much stirring within me, so lovely and still."

"What are you waiting for?" he asked.

"It seems now he'll come back again," she said.

"When, Ellen?"

"I don't know. I just feel that he will." She smiled patiently, with such a depth of certainty and peace that he dared not speak. For many minutes he sat beside her, stirred and wondering. Deep within him was a pain that seemed to be a part of all the years of his own life, but he could really feel nothing but her contentment now. Nothing that had ever happened to him seemed as important as this secret gladness Ellen was sharing with him.

He got up at last and said quietly, "I'll go now, Ellen. Good night."

"Good night, Dad," she said, and he felt that she was smiling.

The Green Hills
by Walter Macken

A young man and a young woman are in love in a small Irish sea-side village. He, though, is ambitious to get on in the world, and there's no scope for his ambition in a tiny place like that. He insists on going in search of success, but will he keep his promise to return?

"What's the use of cryin'?" he asked.

"It makes your eyes sparkle," she said.

"It also makes them red and ugly," he said.

"Well, at léast," she said, "they are my own eyes and I can do what I like with them."

They were silent for a time.

They sat beneath the brow of the green hill. They could see the village below them and the silent sea out beyond as placid as a good dream. The red sun was just about to plunge into the sea. You'd almost listen to hear the sizzling sound it should make. That was on their right. And on their left the moon was in the sky, crescented, its light lit, ready with its feeble but fertile challenge to the departing sun. It was a warm evening. The bracken on which they sat was crinkly dry.

He was leaning back on his elbow, plucking at the fading blossoms of the heather, idly, tearing it with strong brown fingers.

"The village looks nice now from here," he said.

It did. It was small. There were six houses, all newly built inside the last few years. Some of them were plastered with a white cement, some of them roughcast with a cream dash. They sat in a regular half-circle around the small quay. The school was in the middle. The priest came over from the other side to say Mass there on Sundays. It looked nice. You could see four currachs[1] drawn up on the yellow sands and the mast of a hooker, rope festooned, rising from the far side of the quay. There was a dog barking in the street. They were high up on the hill. Over from them, around the shoulder of the hill, a mountain stream rushed down to seek the sea. It didn't rush much now. It wanted rain to make it roar. But you could hear it if you listened for it.

"It looks nice," she said. "I hope you will remember it."

"I know it's nice," he said. "I will probably remember it. But there are bound to be places just as nice as it."

"Do you mean that, now," she asked, "or are you only saying it because you're beginning to feel lonely already?"

Her back was towards him, her head bent. It was a

1 *currach:* a small fishing boat.

a good back, a good strong back, tapering to a narrow waist. Her hair, cut short for utility's sake, was brown with flecks of lighter hair bleached by the sun. He knew her face. It was broad and handsome, well shaped and firm. That was it – firm. Firm eyebrows and a small firm nose and chin with the lips turned out as if they were pursed. Her eyes were startlingly light blue and direct, but they could be soft.

"No," he said, "I'm not getting lonely already. I have been away before."

"But this time you won't be coming back," she said.

"I don't know,' he said. "I might, but I hope I won't be coming back. I hope that if I come back I will come back with money in my pocket which I will spend freely and that I will go away again, and that this time you will come with me."

"No," she said.

"Why, but why?" he asked.

"We've said it all before," she said. "What's the use, Derry?"

"What the hell is there below there," he asked with an impatient sweep of his arm, "that binds you to it?"

"I just like it, that's all," she said. "That's all. I just like it. I like what we have and I don't think anywhere else could be the same as it, and I just like it, that's all."

"How can you know?" he asked. "How in the name of God can you know until you see other places to compare with it? Are you happy to spend your whole life here, growing old and dying and never to have been out of it?"

"I am," she said.

"Well, I'm not," he said decisively. "You talk about the green hills. What green hills? You talk about green hills as if there weren't any green hills anywhere else in the world. There are. I saw them. I saw green hills that'd make this one look like it had the mange." He got up and then stooped and took her hand and pulled her up to face him. He was tall: he looked down at her face. She looked at him. "Didn't I tell you you'd make your eyes red? They are. Listen, Martha, there's just this difference between us. You want to stay here. I want to go away from it. That's the only difference. One of us will have to give way. We know what it means. What it will mean not to be together. I tell you when I come back for you you will forget the green hills."

"There's more between us," she said, looking into the restless eyes. "You have shocking ambition. That's between us. Why can't you be ambitious here? Why do you have to go three thousand miles to be ambitious?"

"Here! What's here?" he asked, breaking away from her. "Nothing. Work, work, work. What you get? You get enough to eat. New suit in a year, a bicycle on the hire purchase. Cycle ten miles to a picture. Six miles to a dance. Year in year out. Gloom in the winter. Fish, shoot. But we're not getting anywhere. We're not just doing anything. I just can't stand it. You know what can happen. I'll get on. I'll get on fast. I have it up here. I'll become somebody. You'll see."

"That's the trouble," she said. "I know you will, and I don't know that you'll be the betther of it." The broad shoulders, the close-cropped hair, the brown strong face and the restless eyes. Oh, he'd get somewhere all right. He was like a big city man at this moment with his well cut double-breasted suit and the white shirt and light shoes looking incongruous on the side of a Connemara hill. He came back to her. He put his big arms around her. She could feel his breath on her face.

"You'll change, my girl," he said. I could change in a minute, she thought, when I am as close to him as this. "You can't whip our feeling. You'll see. I'm willing to put up with it until I come back for you. I'll make that gift to you, the fact that I have to come back to you, that I can't force you to come with me. You wait for me. You take up with any of the lads below and I'll murder them, you'll see. You hear that."

"I do," she said.

They heard his father's voice calling then. He was coming up the hill. He kissed her hard. Her lips were bruised against her teeth. But she strained to him. Almost his heart missed a beat, at the thought that he would be without her. But the restlessness came back to him. A four-engined plane winging over the sea with a gigantic continent below waiting to be conquered by Derry O'Flynn. it would be done. Lesser men had done it before him if they had the sluggish Irish blood that seemed to gush and gurgle with restless achievement once they got away from the inertia of their own villages.

"Goodbye, darling, for now," said Derry.

"Goodbye," she said, her head hiding in his chest.

"There you are," his father said, coming up with the slow loping stride of the shepherd. The dog was with him. He was a big loose-limbed man. In the moonlight you could mistake him for his son if his eyes weren't so quiet. Then where did Derry get the eyes? His mother below was a quiet-eyed woman too.

"There's a few people in below now," the father said. "We better go down to the house."

"I'll go down to them," said Derry. "Let ye come after me. I'll see ye below." And he was gone, bounding down the hill like a goat, sideways and forward and jumping and never missing a step. They stood and watched him becoming smaller and smaller.

"He has a lot of energy," said Derry's father.

"He has a lot of ambition," said Martha, moving off. He looked after her. She was probably crying, he thought. He knew Derry's mother was crying. He wondered idly if the tears of women would make a big river, all the tears of all the women in the world. What good did all those tears do ever? Did they ever soften a heart or deflect a man from a purpose; or if they did, what did their success mean but frustration afterwards? He sighed and caught up with her.

"Going to America is not what it was when I was young," he said as he walked beside her. He admired Martha very much. She could walk down a hill like a healthy sheep.

"It's different," she said.

"Man," he said, "if you were going to America when

I was young, you'd have to be preparing for a year. Everyone within fifty miles knew you were going, and they'd all make sure to see you before you left and wish you away with a tear or a little gift or a holy medal to guard you from the perils of the deep or a good scapular. Now – well, look at it now."

"It's been pepped up," said Martha, smiling. "Isn't it only twelve hours away? It's quicker now to go there than to go to Dublin."

"Spoiled they have it," he said. "Man, we used to have great times at the wakes before they went. We'd all cry our eyes out and we'd dance and drink porter until the small hours of the mornin'. I suppose you can't feel sorry for people now when they're only twelve hours away. Sure they could be only in the next parish."

"You'll miss Derry," she said.

He faltered then, of course.

"Oh, not much," he said. "It's like I'm saying. You haven't time. It's not the same. Besides, Derry was always restless. This is his third time away. Twice before, he was in England. He was always a restless one. I don't know where we got him. Sometimes I say to his mother that she must have been courted by a wandering one on the sly." He chuckled at this. "You should have gone with him, Martha," he said then, gently. "He's very set on you."

"I'm set on him too," she said. "But I'm set on here. I think he should be ambitious at home. It would take little to make me go with him, but it will be better that I don't."

"I know him," said his father. "He will come back for you."

"Maybe by then," she said, "I will have changed, or he will have changed. Let him have his head now, and he will conquer the green hills of America."

"Will you come into the house?" he asked as they paused on the street. "A few of his friends and a few bottles of stout and a few songs. Man, but it's only a ghost of the good wakes long ago."

"I'll go home," she said. "We've said all that's to be

said. I will see him when he comes home."

"All right. Good night, girl. God bless you."

He watched her away. She walked slowly, her head was bent. One hand was behind her holding her other arm. She was idly kicking small stones out of her way. He sighed and turned towards the door of his house. There was no noise coming from it. Somehow this annoyed him. He spoke out loud. "Man, years ago the roof would have been coming off that house with the noise," he said. He went in.

Derry came back for her. Almost a year to the day. But he didn't come alone. He was accompanied by two American sergeants and a firing party of American soldiers, and he had an American flag on his coffin, and his father had a medal that was given to Derry for bravery in some foreign war, and he was planted in the small graveyard halfway up the green hill, right beside the stream that roared when the rain hit the hill and tinkled when it was low. And from here if you stood by his grave to put fresh flowers in the glass jar, you could look out across the wide expanse of the sea; and if you had the vision, miles and miles and miles away you could see the green hills on the other side of the world.

Their Mother's Purse

by Morley Callaghan

Both brother and sister have grown up, left home, and got jobs. Joe sees a new side to his younger sister's character on the night she borrows some money from their parents.

Joe went around to see his mother and father, and while he was talking with them and wondering if he could ask for the loan of a dollar, his sister Mary, who was dressed to go out for the evening, came into the room and said, "Can you let me have fifty cents tonight, Mother?"

She was borrowing money all the time now, and there was no excuse for her, because she was a stenographer[1] and made pretty good pay. It was not the same with her as it was with their older brother, Stephen, who had three children, and could hardly live on his salary.

"If you could possibly spare it, I'd take a dollar," Mary was saying in her low and pleasant voice as she pulled on her gloves. Her easy smile, her assurance that she would not be refused, made Joe feel resentful. He knew that if he had asked for money, he would have shown that he was uneasy and a little ashamed, and that his father would have put down his paper and stared at him and his mother would have sighed and looked dreadfully worried, as though he were the worst kind of spend-thrift.

Getting up to find her purse, their mother said, "I don't mind lending it to you, Mary, though I can't figure out what you do with your money."

"I don't seem to be doing anything with it I didn't use to do," Mary said.

"And I seem to do nothing these days but hand out money to the lot of you. I can't think how you'll get along when I'm dead."

"I don't know what you'd all do if it weren't for your mother's purse," their father said, but when he spoke he nodded his head at Joe, because he would rather make it appear that he was angry with Joe than risk offending Mary by speaking directly to her.

"If anybody wants money, they'll have to find my purse for me," the mother said. "Try and find it, Mary, and bring it to me."

Joe had always thought of Mary as his young sister, but the inscrutable expression he saw on her face as she moved around the room picking up newspapers and looking on chairs made him realize how much more self-reliant, how

1 *stenographer*: shorthand typist.

much apart from them, she had grown in the last few years. He saw that she had become a handsome woman. In her tailored suit and felt hat, she looked almost beautiful, and he was suddenly glad she was his sister.

By this time his mother had got up and was trying to remember where she had put the purse when she came in from the store. In the way of a big woman, she moved around slowly, with a far-away expression in her eyes. The purse was a large, black, flat leather purse, but there never had been a time when his mother had been able to get up and know exactly where her purse was, though she used to pretend she was going directly to the spot where she had placed it.

Now she had got to the point where her eyes were anxious as she tried to remember. Her husband, making loud clucking noises with his tongue, took off his glasses and said solemnly, "I warn you, Mrs McArthur, you'll lose that purse some day, and then there'll be trouble and you'll be satisfied."

She looked at him impatiently, as she had hunted in all the likely corners and cupboards. "See if you can find my purse, will you, son?" she begged Joe, and he got up and began to help, as he used to do when he was a little boy.

Because he remembered that his mother sometimes used to put her purse under the pillow on her bed, he went to look in the bedroom. When he got to the door, which was half closed, and looked in, he saw Mary standing in front of the dresser with their mother's purse in her hands. He saw at once that she had just taken out a bill and was slipping it into her own purse – he even saw that it was a two-dollar bill. He ducked back into the hall before she could catch sight of him. He felt helpless and knew only that he couldn't bear that she should see him.

Mary, coming out of the bedroom, called, "I found it. Here it is, Mother."

"Where did you find it, darling?"

"Under your pillow."

"Ah, that's right. Now I remember," she said, and

looked at her husband triumphantly, for she never failed to enjoy finding the purse just when it seemed to be lost forever.

As Mary handed the purse to her mother, she was smiling, cool, and unperturbed, yet Joe knew she had put the two dollars into her own purse. It seemed terrible that she was able to smile and hide her thoughts like that when they had all been so close together for so many years.

"I never have the slightest fear that it's really lost," the mother said, beaming. Then they watched her, as they had watched her for years after she had found her purse; she was counting the little roll of bills. Her hand went up to her mouth, she looked thoughtful, she looked down into the depths of the purse again, and they waited almost eagerly, as if expecting her to cry out suddenly that the money was not all there. Then, sighing, she took out fifty cents, handed it to Mary, and it was over, and they never knew what she thought.

"Good night, Mother. Good night, Dad," Mary said.

"Good night, and don't be late. I worry when you're late."

"So long, Joe."

"Just a minute," Joe called, and he followed Mary out to the hall. The groping, wondering expression on his mother's face as she counted her money had made him feel savage.

He grabbed Mary by the arm just as she was opening the door.

"Wait a minute," he whispered.

"What's the matter, Joe? You're hurting my arm."

"Give that bill back to them. I saw you take it."

"Joe, I needed it." She grew terribly ashamed and couldn't look at him. "I wouldn't take it if I didn't need it pretty bad," she whispered.

They could hear their father making some provoking remark, and they could hear the easy, triumphant answer of their mother. Without looking up, Mary began to cry a little; then she raised her head and begged in a frightened whisper, "Don't tell them, Joe. Please don't tell them."

"If you needed the money, why didn't you ask them for it?"

"I've been asking for a little nearly every day."

"You only look after yourself, and you get plenty for that."

"Joe, let me keep it. Don't tell them, Joe."

Her hand tightened on his arm as she pleaded with him. Her face was now close against his, but he was so disgusted with her he tried to push her away. When she saw that he was treating her as though she were a cheap crook, she looked helpless and whispered, "I've got to do something. I've been sending money to Paul Farrel."

"Where is he?"

"He's gone to a sanitarium, and he had no money," she said.

In the moment while they stared at each other, he was thinking of the few times she had brought Paul Farrel to their place, and of the one night when they had found out that his lung was bad. They had made her promise not to see him any more, thinking it was a good thing to do before she went any further with him.

"You promised them you'd forget about him," he said.

"I married him before he went away," she said. "It takes a lot to look after him. I try to keep enough out of my pay every week to pay for my lunches and my board here, but I never seem to have enough left for Paul, and then I don't know what to do."

"You're crazy. He'll die on your hands," he whispered. "Or you'll have to go on keeping him."

"He'll get better," she said. "He'll be back in maybe a year." There was such an ardent fierceness in her words, and her eyes shone with such eagerness, that he didn't know what to say to her. With a shy, timid smile, she said, "Don't tell them, Joe."

"O.K.," he said, and he watched her open the door and go out.

He went back to the living-room, where his mother was saying grandly to his father, "Now you'll have to wait till next year to cry blue ruin."

74

His father grinned and ducked his head behind his paper. "Don't worry. There'll soon be a next time," he said.

"What did you want to say to Mary?" his mother asked.

"I just wanted to know if she was going my way, and she wasn't," Joe said.

And when Joe heard their familiar voices and remembered Mary's frightened, eager face, he knew he would keep his promise and say nothing to them. He was thinking how far apart he had grown from them; they knew very little about Mary, but he never told them anything about himself, either. Only his father and mother had kept on going the one way. They alone were still close together.

The Road
by Alan Sillitoe

*Stanley and Amy have been married for some years, and have one
small son called Ivan. Stanley is a waiter in Nottingham, always
rushing and active. Amy works as a cashier, and is slow but bad
tempered. One summer's day they decide to take Ivan to the seaside
to Skegness, where they had spent their honeymoon years before. The
day's experiences bring out all their differences, and lead to argu-
ments. Yet, are they happy together?*

When Ivan was five his parents took him on a day trip to Skegness. They wanted to spend a few hours out of the city and see the coast where they had languished for ten days of a misty frustrating honeymoon of long ago, but Stanley said: "Let's take Ivan to the seaside. It'll do him good."

"Yes," his mother said, "he'll love it."

And Ivan, sucking a lollipop as they walked up Arkwright Street, was oblivious to the responsibility they had put onto his shoulders. Yesterday the car had broken down, so they were going by train. To Stanley everything always happened at the crucial moment, otherwise why did it happen at all?

Ivan wore a new navy blazer, and long trousers specially creased for Whitsun. His shoes were polished and tight around his checked socks. Dark thin hair was well parted, and shy blue eyes looked out of a pale face that tapered from a broad forehead down to his narrow chin and royal blue tie. He held his father with one hand, and gripped his lollipop with the other.

"It'll be marvellous to get to the sea," Stanley said. "It's a hard life being a waiter, and good to have a whole day off for a change."

Amy agreed on all counts, though didn't say so aloud. Ivan wondered if there'd be boats, and she answered that she dare say there would be. Stanley picked Ivan up and put him high on his shoulders: "We'd better hurry."

"You'll have a heart attack if you're not careful," she laughed, "like in them adverts!"

"We've got to get going, though."

"There's still half an hour," she said, "and we're nearly there." Such bleak and common rush seemed to expose her more to the rigours of the world than was necessary, so she would never run, not even for a bus that might make her late for work if she missed it. But then, she never was late for work, and it was part of Stanley's job to get a move on.

He fought his way into the carriage to get seats, and even then Amy had to sit a few rows down. Ivan stayed with his father, now and again standing on his grey flannel trousers for a better view. The carriage was full, and he adjusted quickly to his new home, for all the unfamiliar people in the compartment became part of his family. Strange faces that he would be half afraid of on the street or in dreams seemed now so close and large and smiling, loud in their gaze or talk, that they could not but be uncles and aunts and cousins. In which case he could look with absolute safety at everything outside.

His blue eyes pierced with telescopic clarity the scene of a cow chewing by green indistinct waterbanks of a flooded field that the sky, having been fatally stabbed, had fallen into. A hedge unfurled behind the cow that stood forlorn as if it would be trapped should the water rise further – which it could not do under such moist sunshine.

Gone.

Railway trucks at station sidings fell back along the line like dominoes.

Gone.

An ochred[1] farmhouse came, and stood for a second to show a grey slate roof, damp as if one big patch had settled all over it, the yard around flooded with mud and a man standing in it looking at the train. He waved. Ivan lifted his hand.

Gone.

A junction line vanished into the curve of a cutting.

Gone. All going or gone. They were still, who were gazing out of the windows, and everything was passing them.

The train found its way along, seemed to be making tracks as it went and leaving them brand-new behind, shining brightly when they turned a wide bend and Ivan stretched his neck to look back. An older boy smiled: "Have you seen my new toy?"

He was sullen at being taken from such never-ending pictures that seemed to belong to him. "No."

"Do you want to ?" He put an object on the table,

1 *ochred :* painted a yellow colour.

ovoid,[1] rubber, with four short legs as hands and arms. A length of fine tubing ran from its back to a hollow reservoir of air – which the boy held in his hand. Ivan stared at the rubber, in spite of not wanting to, then at the object on the table that sprang open and up, a horrific miniature skeleton, ready to grow enormously in size and grab everyone in sight, throttle them one and all and send them crushed and raw out of the window – starting with Ivan.

He drew back, and Stanley laughed at his shout of panic, hoping the boy would go on working it so that he too could enjoy the novelty. "Stare at it like a man, then you won't be frightened ! It's only a skeleton."

When the boy held it to Ivan's face, it became the arms and legs of a threatening silver spider brushing his cheeks. Fields rattled by but gave no comfort, so closing his eyes he buried his head against his father. "You are a silly lad. It's only a toy."

"Make him stop it. I don't like it." But he looked again at the glaring death-head, phosphorus[2] on black, shaking and smiling, arms and legs going in and out as if in the grip of some cosmic agony. Amy came along the gangway at his cry and knocked the boy away, daring his nearby mother to object. She took Ivan on her knee: "He was frightening him, you damned fool," she said to Stanley. "Couldn't you see?"

The train stopped at a small station. A gravel depot was heaped between two wooden walls, and beyond the lines a rusting plough grew into an elderberry bush. No one got on or off the train, which made the stop boring and inexplicable. People rustled among baskets and haversacks for sandwiches and flasks of drink.

"I want some water," Ivan said, staring at the open door of the waiting-room.

"You'll have to wait," Amy said.

"There's an hour yet," Stanley reminded her. "He can't."

The train jolted, as if about to start. "I'm thirsty. I want a drink of water."

1 *ovoid*: oval, shaped like an egg.
2 *phosphorus*: glowing white even in the dark.

"O my God," his mother said. "I told you we should have bought some lemonade at the station."

"We had to get straight on. We were late."

"A couple of minutes wouldn't have mattered."

"I wanted to get seats."

"We'd have found some somewhere."

To argue about what was so irrevocably finished infuriated him, but he deliberately calmed himself and rooted in the basket for a blue plastic cup. His whole body was set happily for action: "I'll just nip across to the tap."

"The train's going to start," she said. "Sit down."

"No, it won't." But he didn't get up, paralysed by her objection.

"Are you going?" she said, "or aren't you?" A vein jumped at the side of his forehead as he pushed along the crowded gangway, thinking that if he didn't reach the door and get free of her in a split second he would either go mad or fix his hands at her throat. Their carriage was beyond the platform, and he was out of sight for a moment. Then she saw him running between two trolleys into the men's lavatory as another playful whistle sounded from the engine.

"Where's dad gone, mam?"

"To get some water."

Everyone was looking out of the window, interested in his race: "He won't make it."

"I'll lay a quid each way."

"Don't be bleddy silly, he'll never get back in time. You can hear the wheels squeaking already. Feel that shuddering?"

"You're bleddy hopeful. We'll be here an hour yet." The face disappeared behind a bottle: "I'll live to see us move."

Money was changing hands in fervid betting.

"He will."

"He won't."

At the second whistle he bobbed up, pale and smiling, a cup held high, water splashing over the brim.

"What's dad out there for?" Ivan asked, lifting his face

from a mug of lemonade someone had given him. The wheels moved more quickly, and Stanley was half way along the platform. Odds were lengthening as he dropped from view, and pound notes were flying into the bookie's cap. A woman who wanted to place two bob each way was struggling purple-faced to get from the other end of the carriage. Her coins were passed over.

Amy sat tight-lipped, unwilling to join in common words of encouragement even if it meant never seeing him again. Their return tickets were in his wallet, as well as money and everything else that mattered, but she wouldn't speak. He can wander over the earth till he drops, she thought, though the vision of him sitting outside some charming rustic pub with twelve empty pint jars (and the plastic cup still full of water) in front of him, while she explained at the other end about their lost tickets and destitution didn't make his disappearance too easy to keep calm about.

The carriage slid away, a definite move of steel rolling over steel beneath them all. He was trying not to spill his hard-won water. A roar of voices blasted along the windows as the train gathered speed. "He's missed it!"

The door banged open, and a man who had slept through the betting spree jumped in his seat. He had come off nights at six that morning, and his false teeth jerked so that only a reflex action with both hands held them in the general neighbourhood of his mouth. Red in the face, he slotted them properly in with everyone looking on.

"What's the hurry, you noisy bogger?" he asked, at Stanley standing upright and triumphant beside him.

They clamoured at the bookie to pay up, and when his baffled face promised to be slow in doing so they stopped laughing and threatened to throw him off the bleeding train. He'd seen and grabbed his chance of making a few quid on the excursion, but having mixed up his odds he now looked like being sorted out by the crowd.

"Leave him alone," the winners shouted. But they clapped and cheered, and avoided a fight as the train swayed with speed between fields and spinnies. Stanley stood with the plastic cup two-thirds full then made his way to Ivan and Amy, unable to understand what all the daft excitement was about.

"What did you have to make a laughing-stock of yourself like that for?" she wanted to know.

"He needed some water, didn't he?"

"You mean you had to put on a show for everybody." Their argument went unnoticed in the general share-out. "You can see how much he wanted water," she said, pointing to his closed eyes and hung-down lower lip fixed in sleep.

The sea was nowhere to be seen. They stood on the front and looked for it. Shining sand stretched left and right, and all the way to the horizon, pools and small salt rivers flickered under the sun now breaking through. The immense sky intimidated them, made Skegness seem small at their spines. It looked as if the ocean went on forever round the world and came right back to their heels.

"This is a rum bloody do," he said, setting Ivan down. "I thought we'd take a boat out on it. What a place to build a seaside resort."

She smiled. "You know how it is. The tide'll be in this afternoon. Then I suppose you'll be complaining that all the sand's under water. It's better this way because he can dig and not fall in."

A few people had been on the beach but now, on either side, hundreds advance onto the sand, hair and dresses and white shirts moving against the wind, a shimmering film of blue and grey, red and yellow spreading from the funnel of the station avenue. Campstools and crates of beer staked each claim, and children started an immediate feverish digging as if to find buried toys before the tide came back.

"Can I have a big boat?" Ivan asked as they went closer to the pier and coastguard station. "With a motor in it, and a lot of seats?"

"Where do you want to go?" Stanley asked.

Ivan wondered. "A long way. That's where I want to go. A place like that. Up some road.'

"We'll get you a bus, then," his father laughed.

"You want to stay at home with your mam," she said. They walked further down the sand, between people who had already set out their camps. Neither spoke, or thought of stopping. Gulls came swooping low, their shadows sharp as if to slice open pools of water. "How much more are we going to walk?"

"I didn't know you wanted to stop," he said, stopping.

"I didn't know you wanted to come this far, or I wouldn't have come. You just walk on and on.

"Why didn't you speak up, then?"

"I did. Why didn't you stop?"

"I'm not a mind-reader."

"You don't have to be. You don't even think. Not about other people, anyway."

"I wanted to get beyond all this crowd."

"I suppose you wanted to dump us in the sea."

"I didn't want to sit all day in a café like you did, and that's a fact.'

"You're like a kid, always wanting to be on your own."

"You're too bossy, always wanting your own way."

"It usually turns out to be better than yours. But you never know what you do want, anyway."

He was struck dumb by this irrational leap-frogging argument from someone he blindly loved. He stood and looked at the great space of sand and sky, birds, and a slight moving white beard of foam appearing on the far edge of the sand where the sea lay fallow and sleepy.

"Well?" she demanded. "Are we traipsing much further, or aren't we? I wish you'd make up your mind."

He threw the basket down. "Here's where we stay, you hasty-tempered bitch."

"You can be on your own, then," she said, "because I'm going."

He opened a newspaper, without even bothering to watch her go – which was what she'd throw at him when she came back. "You didn't even watch me go!" He should have been standing up and keeping her retreating figure in sight – that was fast merging with the crowd – his face frowning and unhappy in wondering whether or not he had lost her for ever.

But, after so long, his reactions would not mesh into gear. They'd become a deadeningly smooth surface that struck no sparks any more. When she needed him to put an arm around her and tell her not to get excited – to calm down because he loved her very much – that was when his mouth became ashen and his eyes glazed into the general paralysis of his whole body. She needed him most at the precise moment when he needed her most, and so they retreated into their own damaged worlds to wait for the time when they again felt no need of each other, and they could then give freely all that was no longer wanted, but which was appreciated nevertheless.

"Where's Mam gone?" Ivan asked, half-hidden in his well-dug hole.

"To fetch us something."

"What, though?" .

"We'll see."

"Will she get me a tractor?"

"You never know."

"I want a red one."

"Let's dig a moat," Stanley said, taking the spade. "We'll rig a castle in the middle."

He looked up from time to time, at other people coming to sit nearby. An old man opened a camp-stool and took off his jacket. He wore a striped shirt over his long straight back, braces taut at the shoulders. Adjusting his trilby hat, he looked firmly and unblinking out to sea, so that Stanley paused in his work to see what he was fixing with such determination.

Nothing.

"Shall we make a tunnel, Dad?"

"All right, then, but it'll crumble."

The thin white ray was coming towards them, feather-tips lifting from it, a few hundred yards away and suddenly no longer straight, pushed forward a little in the centre, scarred by the out-jutting pier. It broke on the sand and went right back.

"She'll be in in a bit; don't worry. We're in the front line, so we'll have to move," the old man said. "Half an hour at the most. You can't stop it, and that's a fact. Comes in shoulder-high, faster than a racehorse sometimes, and then you've got to watch out, even from this distance, my guy you have. Might look a fair way and flat one minute, then it's marching in quick like the Guards. Saw a man dragged in once, big six-footer he was. His wife and kids just watched. Found 'im in the Wash a week later. Pulls you underfoot. Even I can find my legs and run at times like that, whether I'm eighty or not."

If it weren't for the trace of white he'd hardly have known where sky ended and sand began, for the wetness of it under the line was light purple, a mellower shade of the midday lower horizon. The mark of white surf stopped them blending, a firm and quite definite dividing of earth and water and air.

"Come here every year, then?" Stanley asked.

"Most days," the man said. "Used to be a lifeboatman. I live here." His hand ran around the inside of a straw basket like a weasel and pulled out a bottle of beer. He untwisted the tight cork, up-ended it, and swigged it into his bony throat. "You from Notts, I suppose?"

Stanley nodded. "I'm a waiter. Wangled some time off for a change. It don't make so much difference at a big hotel. There used to be a shortage, but we've got some of them Spanish chaps now." His jacket and tie lay on the sand, one sleeve hidden by a fallen rampart of Ivan's intricate castle.

Looking up he saw Amy making her way between patchwork blankets of people, a tall and robust figure wearing a flowered dress. A tied ribbon set hair spreading towards her shoulders. She never tried to look fabricated and smart, even on her job as a cashier at the local dance hall. He was almost annoyed at being so happy to see her, yet finally gave in to his pleasure and watched her getting closer, while hoping she had now recovered from her fits of the morning. Perhaps the job she had was too much for her, but she liked to work, because it gave a feeling of independence, helped to keep that vitality and anger that held Stanley so firmly to her. It was no easy life, and because of the money she earned little time could be given to Ivan, though such continual work kept the family more stable than if as a triangle the three of them were too much with each other – which they wanted to be against their own and everyone's good.

She had sandwiches, fried fish, cakes, dandelion-and-burdock, beer. "This is what we need to stop us feeling so rattled."

He wondered why she had to say the wrong thing so soon after coming back. "Who's rattled?"

"You were. I was as well, if you like. Let's eat this though. I'm starving."

She opened the packets, and kept them in equal radius around her, passing food to them both. "I didn't know how hungry I was," Stanley said.

"If anything's wrong," she said, "it's usually that – or something else." She reached out, and they pressed each other's hand.

"You look lovely today," he said.

"I'm glad we came."

"So am I. Maybe I'll get a job here."

"It'd be seasonal," she said. "Wouldn't do for us."

"That's true."

While Ivan had his mouth full of food, some in his hand, and a reserve waiting in his lap, she asked if he wanted any more. Even at home, when only half-way through a plate, the same thing happened, and Stanley wondered whether she wanted to stuff, choke or stifle him – or just kill his appetite. He'd told her about it, but it made no difference.

After the meal Ivan took his bread and banana and played at the water's edge, where spume spread like silver shekels in the sun and ran around his plimsolls, then fell back or faded into the sand. He stood up, and when it tried to catch him he ran, laughing so loudly that his face turned as red as the salmon paste spread on the open rolls that his mother and father were still eating. The sea missed him by inches. The castle-tumulus of sand was mined and sapped by salt water until its crude formations became lop-sided, a boat rotted by time and neglect. A sudden up-surge melted it like wax, and on the follow-up there was no trace. He watched it, wondering why it gave in so totally to such gentle pressure.

They had to move, and Amy picked up their belong-ings, unable to stop water running over the sleeve of Stanley's jacket. "You see," she chided, "if you hadn't in-sisted on coming all this way. down we wouldn't have need-ed to shift so early."

He was sleepy and good-natured, for the food hadn't yet started to eat his liver. "Everybody'll have to move. It goes right up to the road when it's full in."

"Not for another twenty minutes. Look how far down we are. Trust us to be in the front line. That's the way you like it, though. If only we could do something right for a change, have a peaceful excursion without much going wrong."

He thought so, too, and tried to smile as he stood up to help.

"If everything went perfectly right one day," she said, "you'd still have to do something and deliberately muck it up, I know you would."

As he said afterwards – or would have said if the same course hadn't by then been followed yet again – one thing led to another, and before I could help myself...

The fact was that the whole acreage of the remaining sands, peopled by much of Nottingham on its day's outing, was there for an audience, or would have been if any eyes had been trained on them, which they weren't particularly. But many of them couldn't help but be, after the first smack. In spite of the sea and the uprising wind, it could be heard, and the second was indeed listened for after her raging cry at the impact.

"You tried me," he said, hopelessly baffled and above all immediately sorry. "You try me all the time." And the jerked-out words, and the overwhelming feeling of regret, made him hit her a third time, till he stood, arms hanging thinly at his side like the maimed branches of some blighted and thirsty tree that he wanted to disown but couldn't. They felt helpless, and too weak to be kept under sufficient control. He tried to get them safely into his pockets, but they wouldn't fit.

A red leaf-mark above her eye was slowly swelling. "Keep away," she cried, lifting her heavy handbag but unable to crash it against him. She sobbed. It was the first time he had hit her in public, and the voices calling that he should have less on it, and others wondering what funny stuff she had been up to to deserve it, already sounded above the steady railing of the nerve-racking sea. An over-forward wave sent a line of spray that saturated one of her feet. She ignored it, and turned to look for Ivan among the speckled colours of the crowd. Pinks and greys, blues and whites shifted across her eyes and showed nothing.

She turned to him: "Where is he, then?"

He felt sullen and empty, as if he were the one who'd been hit. "I don't know. I thought he was over there."

"Where?"

"Just there. He was digging."

"O my God, what if he's drowned?"

"Don't be so bloody silly," he said, his face white, and thinner than she'd ever seen it. Bucket and spade lay by the basket between them. They looked into the sea, and then towards land, unable to find him from their mutual loathing and distress. They were closer than anyone else to the sea, and the old lifeboatman had gone. Everyone had moved during their argument, and the water now boiled and threw itself so threateningly that they had to pick up everything and run.

"What effect do you think all this arguing and fighting's going to have on him?" she demanded. He'd never thought about such outside problems, and considered she had only mentioned them now so as to get at him with the final weapon of mother-and-child, certainly not for Ivan's own and especial good. Yet he was not so sure. The horror of doubt came over him, opened raw wounds not only to himself but to the whole world for the first time as they walked towards the road and set out on a silent bitter search through the town.

For a long while Ivan sat on the steps of a church, the seventh step down from the doors, beating time with a broken stick as blocks of traffic sped by. He sang a song, dazed, enclosed, at peace. A seagull sat at his feet, and when he sneezed it flew away. He stayed at peace even after they found him, and went gladly on the train with them as if into the shambles. They seemed happily united in getting him back at last. The effort of the search had taken away all their guilt at having succumbed to such a pointless quarrel in front of him. He watched the fields, and heavy streams like long wavy mirrors that cows chewed at and clouds flowed over and ignored.

He sat on his father's knee, who held him as if he were a rather unusual but valuable tip a customer in the restaurant had left. Ivan felt nothing. The frozen soul, set in ancestry and childhood, fixed his eyes to look and see beyond them and the windows. The train wasn't moving after a while. He was sleeping a great distance away from it, detached, its jolting a permanent feature of life and the earth. He wanted to go on travelling forever, as if should he ever stop the sky would fall in. He dreamed that it had, and was about to black him out, so he woke up and clung to his father, asking when they would be back in Nottingham.

The Berry Holly

by Sid Chaplin

His mother and father have parted, and Christmas is near. The boy desperately wants his parents together again. It seems that the man also wants to come back to his wife – at least he has come to find his son and to ask where his mother is.

Mother and boy were going out to gather Christmas holly in the wood near the Durham village where they live. The boy's mother seems fond of the man, but the father's love for his greyhound and his lust for gambling seems to be between them. Will the boy get his father back? It seems to depend on that greyhound.

All alone in the hen-run above Nutty Hag Row the boy worked hard at plucking the chickens, which his grandfather had killed before going off to his afternoon shift in the drift mine which hummed and jangled at the end of the street.

The old stove was cherry red, heating the water which, poured over the chickens, made them easier to pluck. But still it was hard work, and cold, as the feathers flew. After every third chicken he allowed himself a rest, straightening his back and letting his eye rove.

First he looked over the depot where coal streamed into the big-wheeled cowcarts while the shire horses' stamped and blew, then along the curve of the red-roofed street to the river, very deep and black under the lea of the steep wooded hill where the old dam held it back, then widening and becoming white-flecked where the stepping-stones were that led to old Jawblades pit, so near and yet so far away.

There the countryside opened out and with it the sky, awesomely wide and cold with pink combs of cloud, and the sun red and very remote. In his second pause his heart gave a leap at the sight of a man crossing the river, preceded by a greyhound. The man moved hesitantly and clumsily, but the greyhound was fluid, stepping out delicately and smoothly, flowing over the stones.

Because of what Jawblades meant to the boy he cheated and kept constant watch on the pair as they advanced along the riverside path, the dog ranging freely ahead and sometimes streaking across the stubbled fields or sniffing in hedgerows, the man trudging with his head down, deep in thought. When he lost them he grieved. Then he forgot himself in the work.

Suddenly there came a scraping and he turned to find the greyhound reared high on her hind legs as if set to climb, lapping and looking through the penfold with large intelligent eyes.

And there was his father standing with his legs apart and his hands in his pockets, his jacket bulging at one side, his smile lopsided as well. "You've got a shippin' order there," he remarked and came through. The grey-hound whinged. "Settle!" said the man, and the dog immediately lay down on the frost-encrusted grass with her chin between her paws. The man silently took the other pail from the stove and set to, plucking two birds to the boy's one. The chickens drawn and hung in the scrubbed shed, the man lit a cigarette. "Your Mam around?" he asked casually.

"She's at Auntie Polly's," said the boy. "We're goin' to gather berry holly." The man upturned a bucket and smoked broodingly. "Mind if I come with ye?" he asked at last; and the boy smiled. "Then say nowt to your Grandma," said the man. "We'll meet at the end of the street."

The man was waiting, not at the end of the street as promised but along the gleaming tub-track, just at the bend where the rope passed around a guide wheel. They trudged between the rails silently.

When the footpath diverged away from the black deep hole in the rockface the man took the boy's hand and helped him up the steep slope. They went through the five-barred gate with ice tears hanging on the undersides of the cross-bars, past Hutchinson's farm where the cattle in the home field surged towards them, then followed the road as it wound and dropped darkly into Bellburn Wood; and only then did the man relinquish the boy's hand.

In the distance was the old air-shaft and the two cottages, in one of which lived Aunt Polly. "Go on," said the man. "I'll meet you at the berry holly."

"Should Ah – should Ah tell her?" The man shrugged and turned into the wood, the greyhound ranging ahead and snuffling in the heaped leaves under the trees. When the boy arrived, dragging his mother by the hand, he had already cut several grand sprays of holly thick with scarlet berry. "Oh, you've left none for us!" said the boy; and the man smiled and handed him the knife he had been using, a heavy horn-handled knife with a corkscrew, as well as the large curved shining blade.

"Ah've left you some on the bottom branches," he said. "Golly, that's a good knife!" said the boy and started looking for sprays, ducking in and out of the great umbrella-like spread of the holly bush.

"Well, and what brings you here?" he heard his mother say.

"Thought it'd be nice to get the holly berry, same as we used to." said the man, adding with a rush: "And mebbe spend Christmas together."

"You've got a hope, indeed you have," said the woman bitterly; and the boy's heart gave a thump. "We're settled and comfortable – and at least we're *thought of* – not put next to a thing like that!" she concluded with a swift pure look of hate at the dog.

"You could be boss in your house," he said, and in spite of herself her eyes shone. "Ah've never had a better cavil. The money's good. Ah'll turn a fresh leaf. Ah'll get rid of the dog," said the man passionately.

"Get rid of the dog," she mocked. "It'd soon find its way back – and so would the master – back to the gamblin', the boozin' an' the rest of it. And then what? We'd sharp be back on our beam ends again..."

"Ah mean it this time, lass!" he broke in urgently. He looked at the greyhound with a queer, wild kind of desperation. "Ah've run her for the last time. Ah've made a packet and squared off with the lenders. It's a clean start..."

"It'll need some thinkin' about," she said, darkly brooding.

"It's now or never," he said, stooping to gather the berry holly. They went back through the dark wood and dusk was falling as they neared Aunt Polly's. The dusk was setting in, but the berries stood out among the glossy green leaves, perfectly round and blood scarlet among the needle points.

At the air-shaft the man stopped. "Here, lad, take these," he said, handing over his burden of berry holly. "Ah'll wait here."

"You might as well come in and have a cup of tea," urged the woman, in a softer tone than she had hitherto used. But the man shook his head. "Ah'll be waitin' here," he told them.

As the boy followed his mother into the house he heard a sharp whistle and looked back to see the man kneeling by the old air-shaft. The light was smoke-blue and all was quiet. His father was reaching into the bulky poacher's pocket of his jacket. The greyhound came running, then stopped. His father spoke caressingly and she went strangely to him, not sinuously in her own proud way but drag-legged with her ears laid back.

He heard his father murmur something, softly, as the creature came near. Then he went into the bright warmth of Aunt Polly's kitchen, and marvelled at the way the streamers all gold and red stretched out from the mistletoe, which hung like a great glowing bush upside down from the ceiling, with pears and apples of gold and silver bright upon it.

The dull clap came plain, and Aunt Polly paused with the cup at her lips. "It'll be old Hutchinson and his lads after a bit of something for Christmas," said she. "Such demons with guns!"

The boy and his mother looked at each other. Then flushing and with a glance at Aunt Polly, she said: "Go and bring your father. Go, canny lad." He needed no second bidding.

His father was standing with his face against the air-shaft wall, and his arms hung straight down. There was no sign of the dog, but on the frost-encrusted grass little red globules shone. He stooped to touch, and his father turned. "Don't touch, lad!"

Then, wiping one hand on the wall, he said. "Ah couldn't let her die hard – now could Ah?" Not understanding, the boy said yes. What filled *his* mind was that they were together again. But long afterwards it all came back – the dog swift to run, the holly berry on the ground, and a man that turned his face to the wall, and cried. Then he saw what a fortunate child he was, and what manner of father he had, and knew what the berry holly meant, the berry and the thorns.

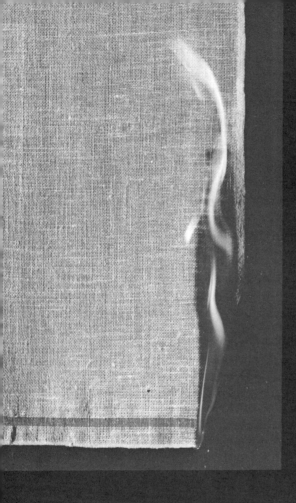

Fire

by Philip Callow

A young man has a first job in a factory. Forced to go home for the day by a power cut, he offers a little help to his mother: the result is frightening.

It was the year of the great freeze, when the whole country lay frozen. The cold had shut down the factory. Something had killed the power, there were rumours of an explosion, but no one really knew. We all arrived as usual, flowing to the entrances from several directions, but then we milled about, baulked, a disorderly flock which grew steadily larger, full of angry noise, with cycles and engines jammed in our midst, as the works police turned us back. Only those at the very front could hear properly. There was a great deal of confusion.

I was on foot that day, because of the state of the roads. There had been successive falls of snow, week after week, each one freezing hard and being hammered down with wheels next day in the streets, then another layer dropping soundlessly through the night. Before long they were having to use pneumatic drills on it, as if they were splitting concrete. That was in the town centre. Out here nothing was done. The buses rocked along dangerously and grew less in number, always packed tight inside, grinding up the hills. It was safer to walk.

"Shove off home, go on, have a holiday," the police were bawling from the gates, enjoying themselves. "Nothing doing here. Breakdown."

It was afternoon. The snow hung overhead, slung in folds all over the brown sky, which was dark with weight.

Trudging back the way I had come, I met a pal at the crossroads who was going in.

"Don't bother yourself, Ralph," I sang out happily, "we've been turned away·– no power."

"No what?" he said, stopping.

"Power gone."

"How's that?"

I shrugged. The icy wind whirled between us, flinging about. It was no place for a chat. Stamping my feet and trying to draw my chin into my overcoat collar, I asked him: "Coming down the road, or d'you fancy waiting for a bus?"

"What *you* going to do?"

He was stiff-necked, bony, about a year older than me,

a bit of black moustache showing thinly on his lip. He played the clarinet.

"Walk," I said. "How about you?"

He suddenly marched forward, in a tremendous hurry. "Come on, then," he rapped, as if he had made the decision long ago, and was persuading me. "It's too bloody cold to hang around." He was like that.

We went along at a good speed. I kept inspiring myself with the thought of this cold, which I felt now to be a thing of enormous roots. It had taken root in the factory. As we swung down to the expanse of white common, where the wandering paths had been all obliterated, the ragged bushes made pretty with tufts of snow, the rough posts standing up stark and significant, our blood moving and warming us, plumes of breath at our mouths, I was looking at everything with gloating, jubilant glances. Men were trailing behind and ahead, black figures mesmerised on themselves, all the different feet crunching busily over the scabs and ruts of the unrecognisable pavements. The whole situation exhilarated me, and I could see by my friend's face that he was feeling the same. He stayed silent, hogging his satisfaction to himself, making the most of it, as I was. Neither of us wanted to talk.

We left the houses behind and the smoke oozing reluctantly from the chimneys, and went out over the grey trampled road-edge, on the flat common. To either side it looked savage and glaring white, unmarked, as if people feared to touch it. We followed the poles that went stalking across, their thin wires biting into the sky.

The ranks of houses on the far side came closer. Then we were there, at the spot where the town really began, the roads crossing and sloping downhill in two directions. Mine was the left branch. We stood a moment, sharp whips of wind on our skins, and the hard blasts that you could feel now and then striking up under the peak of your cap and flattening your trousers.

"So long, then," I said, edging away. I lifted my hand.

"What happens now?" Ralph said, and it was like a shudder. He was hissing between his set teeth, his face blue.

Both of us were jigging on our toes and whacking our hips.

"Why?" I said, stupid with cold.

"Do we go in tomorrow, or what?"

I shook my head violently.

"Somebody said they might sack us all till they got going again – so they don't have to pay for idle time."

"That right?"

"I heard somebody say that – "

"The bastards!"

"You know them."

"The slimy, slippery – "

"Nobody knows for certain what's happening, if you ask me."

"Christ," he said thoughtfully, shrugging and banging away like a machine. The wind cut at my face.

"See you later, Ralph," I said loudly, moving to the left. He nodded and went off without another word, hunched up, his head bowed.

At home, my mother was at the kitchen table, which had been dragged away from the wall. She stood ironing, taking long, hurried strokes, her face red. A half-loaded clothes-horse gaped open, nearly as tall as her, scenting the warm air.

"They've shut down," I muttered fumbling with my buttons.

"Isn't it dreadful, you look frozen stiff – go and sit by the fire, it's lovely and warm in there. Go on in, I'll bring you a hot drink – what did you say?" she said, all in one breath and hardly looking up, the iron still shooting across.

"No electricity – broken down," I shouted through from the living-room.

"What are you talking about? Where?"

"The factory."

"Oh, the factory."

I listened to the rubbing and bumping, as I blew on my dead fingers. Then she called. "I shouldn't go too near that fire, you'll get hot-aches. Wait till I bring you a drink, the kettle's on. Broken down?"

Later, after I had thawed and could use my fingers,

and sat swallowing the tea, sinking my nose over the steam, she came struggling in with the full clothes-horse. I got up.

"Give it me," I said shortly, resisting my tenderness. I gripped the unpainted frame manfully.

"Careful," she said.

"Where d'you want it? How near?"

I set it round the fire.

"Yes, like that. A bit nearer, if you like. You can watch it for me."

She hurried away to the kitchen, to clear up and begin something else.

A few minutes passed. I got up and ran upstairs to find a book. I sat on the bed with it a moment, turning the cold pages. Then a terrible cry from my mother below filled the house with horror.

"Oh God, oh God, quick, quick!" she was shrieking.

The fear rushed through my veins. It drove me out of the bedroom, sweating, carried me along blindly, and I found myself downstairs. My mother stood coughing, her eyes terrified. Even then the smell did not convey anything. She had a bundle of smouldering linen between her hands, held away from her.

"In there – it's on fire – open the kitchen door – oh God, no, don't go in, I don't want you to go in, I don't want anybody else to touch it!" she screamed, blundering past me into the frozen yard. I stared in horror at her awful, distracted face.

When I went in, the living-room was dark as night, full of dense, slowly-rolling brown smoke, and at the far side, where the fireplace was blotted out, I could see a big dimly-glowing mass. There was a terrifying stench, like that of rags burning on a refuse tip. Still trembling with shock, I groped in and found the clothes-horse.

I snatched things off, ruined shirts and vests, tea-towels, and went rushing into the yard. I ran down the path to the frozen garden and tried to dig snow off the flower-beds with my fingers, to use that. But it was all congealed and useless.

"Couldn't you smell it?" my mother moaned, each time I passed her. "Oh, why didn't you, surely you must have been able to smell it!"

I had never seen her like this. She was looking right through me. She seemed a long way off, swallowed up in her racking distress, being trampled and broken, wailing in anguish. I was afraid of her.

The wind had dropped now. When I took a bowl and threw water on the charred, smoking heap of washing, there was a loud hiss, and then the steam rose dismally in a slow cloud, hanging about over the ground.

My mother could not keep still. She kept wandering up and down, sobbing, dragging at her apron with convulsive, demented movements.

"My house – ruined – all the clothes – the room just decorated..." She leaned against the wall and cried weakly, with wide-staring eyes. I was very frightened, and sick with guilt and misery.

"I thought you were in the room," she quavered. She seemed to come back, and her crying stopped. "Where did you go?" she asked, almost calmly.

I struggled to answer, but her shoulders shook and she sobbed again.

"Sit down, Mum, come and sit down," I said, in a barren voice, going up to her. It was an effort to move. I touched her arm fearfully.

"No, no – leave me alone!" she broke out, wailing. She covered her face. Her hair was all loose. She became hysterical, queer sounds shaking out of her.

I stood drearily, watching. This was the first house we had owned. It was not bought even now, but all my father's savings were in it. It represented years of accumulation and struggle, a whole lifetime. My mother was a woman who loved order and cleanliness, things in their places. A home absorbed her whole life, every passion she had; she kept nothing back. Without being told anything I understood how ghastly the disaster was, how enormous and terrifying. I did not know what to do. I hung my head, drained of strength, beaten down by the sight of this grief. It entered all the world, ran into each corner, numbing it, making it black. Looking at her small, pitiful figure, her tangled hair, her face smudged with dirt, tear-stained and swollen, I felt my heart wrung and emptied. The very thought of life overwhelmed me with sickness; I did not want to live. What was the use of life, what did it amount to? It was only an agony. And it seemed incredible that only an hour or two ago I was walking glad with freedom across the raw common, animated and pleased in the whiteness, liking things.

My uncle arrived. By then my mother was slumped in a kitchen chair, exhausted, her expression quite blank and dead. My uncle bent over her with his kind, worried face and his shy hands. He had a speechless, workman's tenderness. Feelings were painful, difficult, and refused to flow into speech. He stood helpless, a good man, smelling of the cold.

"Any brandy?" he asked me softly. I went to look, but my mother was moving her head and trying to speak. "No," she whispered.

"No?" my uncle said, bending lower.

He decided to survey the damage, following me about. One layer of clothes was completely ruined, but when the smoke had gone away the room itself seemed unharmed. There were no marks on the ceiling. The hearth-rug had a large hole eaten from the centre, where a burning table-cloth had dropped down.

He murmured that he would have to leave. He was a night-worker. Going down to the gate he met my father, who stopped to exchange words, then came in differently, with a sharpened face.

"It might have been much worse," my father kept repeating doggedly like a refrain all that evening, before I went out.

The Sniper
by Liam O'Flaherty

There is civil war in the Irish city of Dublin, during the 1930s. The Republicans are fighting the "Free Staters". A Republican sniper on a roof-top is going to face the consequences of the fighting.

The long June twilight faded into night. Dublin lay enveloped in darkness, but for the dim light of the moon, that shone through fleecy clouds, casting a pale light as of approaching dawn over the streets and the dark waters of the Liffey. Around the beleaguered Four Courts the heavy guns roared. Here and there through the city machine guns and rifles broke the silence of the night, spasmodically, like dogs barking on lone farms. Republicans and Free States were waging civil war.

On a roof-top near O'Connel Bridge, a Republican sniper lay watching. Beside him lay his rifle and over his shoulders were slung a pair of field-glasses. His face was the face of a student – thin and ascetic, but his eyes had the cold gleam of the fanatic. They were deep and thoughtful, the eyes of a man who is used to looking at death.

He was eating a sandwich hungrily. He had eaten nothing since morning. He had been too excited to eat. He finished the sandwich, and taking a flask of whiskey from his pocket, he took a short draught. Then he returned the flask to his pocket. He paused for a moment, considering whether he should risk a smoke. It was dangerous. The flash might be seen in the darkness and there were enemies watching. He decided to take the risk. Placing a cigarette between his lips, he struck a match, inhaled the smoke hurriedly and put out the light. Almost immediately, a bullet flattened itself against the parapet of the roof. The sniper took another wiff and put out the cigarette. Then he swore softly and crawled away to the left.

Cautiously he raised himself and peered over the parapet. There was a flash and a bullet whizzed over his head. He dropped immediately. He had seen the flash. It came from the opposite side of the street.

He rolled over the roof to a chimney stack in the rear, and slowly drew himself up behind it, until his eyes were level with the top of the parapet. There was nothing to be seen – just the dim outline of the opposite housetop against the blue sky. His enemy was under cover.

Just then an armoured car came across the bridge and advanced slowly up the street. It stopped on the opposite side of the street fifty yards ahead. The sniper could hear the dull panting of the motor. His heart beat faster. It was an enemy car. He wanted to fire, but he knew it was useless. His bullets would never pierce the steel that covered the grey monster.

Then round the corner of a side street came an old woman, her head covered by a tattered shawl. She began to talk to the man in the turret of the car. She was pointing to the roof where the sniper lay. An informer.

The turret opened. A man's head and shoulders appeared, looking towards the sniper. The sniper raised his rifle and fired. The head fell heavily on the turret wall. The woman darted toward the side street. The sniper fired again. The woman whirled round and fell with a shriek into the gutter.

Suddenly from the opposite roof a shot rang out and the sniper dropped his rifle with a curse. The rifle clattered to the roof. The sniper thought the noise would wake the dead. He stopped to pick the rifle up. He couldn't lift it. His forearm was dead. "Christ," he muttered, "I'm hit."

Dropping flat on to the roof, he crawled back to the parapet. With his left hand he felt the injured right forearm. The blood was oozing through the sleeve of his coat. There was no pain – just a deadened sensation, as if the arm had been cut off.

Quickly he drew his knife from his pocket, opened it on the breastwork of the parapet and ripped open the sleeve. There was a small hole where the bullet had entered. On the other side there was no hole. The bullet had lodged in the bone. It must have fractured it. He bent the arm below the wound. The arm bent back easily. He ground his teeth to overcome the pain.

Then, taking out his field dressing, he ripped open the packet with his knife. He broke the neck of the iodine bottle and let the bitter fluid drip into the wound. A paroxysm of pain swept through him. He placed the cotton wadding over the wound and wrapped the dressing over it. He tied the end with his teeth.

Then he lay still against the parapet, and closing his

eyes, he made an effort of will to overcome the pain.

In the street beneath all was still. The armoured car had retired speedily over the bridge, with the machine gunner's head hanging lifeless over the turret. The woman's corpse lay still in the gutter.

The sniper lay for a long time nursing his wounded arm and planning escape. Morning must not find him wounded on the roof. The enemy on the opposite roof covered his escape. He must kill that enemy and he could not use his rifle. He had only a revolver to do it. Then he thought of a plan.

Taking off his cap, he placed it over the muzzle of his rifle. Then he pushed the rifle slowly upwards over the parapet, until the cap was visible from the opposite side of the street. Almost immediately there was a report, and a bullet pierced the centre of the cap. The sniper slanted the rifle forward. The cap slipped down into the street. Then, catching the rifle in the middle, the sniper dropped his left hand over the roof and let it hang, lifelessly. After a few moments he let the rifle drop to the street. Then he sank to the roof, dragging his hand with him.

Crawling quickly to the left, he peered up at the corner of the roof. His ruse had succeeded. The other sniper seeing the cap and rifle fall, thought that he had killed his man. He was now standing before a row of chimney pots, looking across, with his head clearly silhouetted against the western sky.

The Republican sniper smiled and lifted his revolver above the edge of the parapet. The distance was about fifty yards – a hard shot in the dim light, and his right arm was paining him like a thousand devils. He took a steady aim. His hand trembled with eagerness. Pressing his lips together, he took a deep breath through his nostrils and fired. He was almost deafened with the report and his arm shook with the recoil.

Then, when the smoke cleared, he peered across and uttered a cry of joy. His enemy had been hit. He was reeling over the parapet in his death agony. He struggled to keep his feet, but he was slowly falling forward, as if in a dream. The rifle fell from his grasp, hit the parapet, fell over, bounded off the pole of a barber's shop beneath and then cluttered on to the pavement.

Then the dying man on the roof crumpled up and fell forward. The body turned over and over in space and hit the ground with a dull thud. Then it lay still.

The sniper looked at his enemy falling and he shuddered. The lust of battle died in him. He became bitten by remorse. The sweat stood out in beads on his forehead. Weakened by his wound and the long summer day of fasting and watching on the roof, he revolted from the sight of the shattered mass of his dead enemy. His teeth chattered. He began to gibber to himself, cursing the war, cursing himself, cursing everybody.

He looked at the smoking revolver in his hand and with an oath he hurled it to the roof at his feet. The revolver went off with the concussion, and the bullet whizzed past the sniper's head. He was frightened back to his senses by the shock. His nerves steadied. The cloud of fear scattered from his mind and he laughed.

Taking the whiskey flask from his pocket, he emptied it at a draught. He felt reckless under the influence of the spirits. He decided to leave the roof and look for his company commander to report. Everywhere around was quiet. There was not much danger in going through the streets. He picked up his revolver and put it in his pocket. Then he crawled down through the skylight to the house underneath.

When the sniper reached the laneway on the street level, he felt a sudden curiosity as to the identity of the enemy sniper whom he had killed. He decided that he was a good shot whoever he was. He wondered if he knew him. Perhaps he had been in his own company before the split in the army. He decided to risk going over to have a look at him. He peered around the corner into O'Connell street. In the upper part of the street there was heavy firing, but around here all was quiet.

The sniper darted across the street. A machine gun tore up the ground around him with a hail of bullets, but he escaped. He threw himself face downwards beside the corpse. The machine gun stopped.

Then the sniper turned over the dead body and looked into his brother's face.

The Case for the Defence

by Graham Greene

*A reporter goes to a murder trial at the Central Criminal Court.
It seems to everybody absolutely certain that the accused is certainly
guilty. Convicted murderers were still hanged in this country at the
time the story was written. Such an experienced reporter thinks he
knows exactly how the trial will go. But he is proved wrong.*

It was the strangest murder trial I ever attended. They named it the Peckham murder in the headlines, though Northwood Street, where the old woman was found battered to death, was not strictly speaking in Peckham. This was not one of those cases of circumstantial evidence[1] in which you feel the jurymen's anxiety – because mistakes *have* been made – like domes of silence muting the court. No, this murderer was all but found with the body; no one present when the Crown counsel[2] outlined his case believed that the man in the dock stood any chance at all.

He was a heavy stout man with bulging bloodshot eyes. All his muscles seemed to be in his thighs. Yes, an ugly customer, one you wouldn't forget in a hurry – and that was an important point because the Crown proposed to call four witnesses who hadn't forgotten him, who had seen him hurrying away from the little red villa in Northwood Street. The clock had just struck two in the morning.

Mrs Salmon in 15 Northwood Street had been unable to sleep; she heard a door click shut and thought it was her own gate. So she went to the window and saw Adams (that was his name) on the steps of Mrs Parker's house. He had just come out and he was wearing gloves. He had a hammer in his hand and she saw him drop it into the laurel bushes by the front gate. But before he moved away, he had looked up – at her window. The fatal instinct that tells a man when he is watched exposed him in the light of a street-lamp to her gaze – his eyes suffused with horrifying and brutal fear, like an animal's when you raise a whip. I talked afterwards to Mrs Salmon, who naturally after the astonishing verdict went in fear herself. As I imagine did all the witnesses – Henry MacDougall, who had been driving home from Benfleet late and nearly ran Adams down at the corner of Northwood Street. Adams was walking in the middle of the road looking dazed. And old Mr Wheeler, who lived next door to Mrs Parker, at No. 12, and was wakened by a noise – like a chair falling –

1 *circumstantial evidence*: evidences of the circumstances without the person actually having been witnessed.
2 *Crown counsel*: the barrister or lawyer presenting the case against the accused.

through the thin-as-paper villa wall, and got up and looked out of the window, just as Mrs Salmon had done, saw Adams's back and, as he turned, those bulging eyes. In Laurel Avenue he had been seen by yet another witness — his luck was badly out; he might as well have committed the crime in broad daylight.

"I understand," counsel said, "that the defence proposes to plead mistaken identity. Adams's wife will tell you that he was with her at two in the morning on February 14, but after you have heard the witnesses for the Crown and examined carefully the features of the prisoner, I do not think you will be prepared to admit the possibility of a mistake."

It was all over, you would have said, but the hanging.

After the formal evidence had been given by the police-man who had found the body and the surgeon who examined it, Mrs Salmon was called. She was the ideal witness, with her slight Scotch accent and her expression of honesty, care and kindness.

The counsel for the Crown brought the story gently out. She spoke very firmly. There was no malice in her, and no sense of importance at standing there in the Central Criminal Court with a judge in scarlet hanging on her words and the reporters writing them down. Yes, she said, and then she had gone downstairs and rung up the police station.

"And do you see the man here in court?"

She looked straight at the big man in the dock, who stared hard at her with his pekingese eyes without emotion.

"Yes," she said, "there he is."

"You are quite certain?"

She said simply, "I couldn't be mistaken, sir."

It was all as easy as that.

"Thank you, Mrs Salmon."

Counsel for the defence rose to cross-examine. If you had reported as many murder trials as I have, you would have known beforehand what line he would take. And I was right, up to a point.

"Now, Mrs Salmon, you must remember that a man's life may depend on your evidence."

"I do remember it, sir."

"Is your eyesight good?"

"I have never had to wear spectacles, sir."

"You are a woman of fifty-five?"

"Fifty-six, sir."

"And the man you saw was on the other side of the road?"

"Yes, sir."

"And it was two o'clock in the morning. You must have remarkable eyes, Mrs Salmon?"

"No, sir. There was moonlight, and when the man looked up, he had the lamplight on his face."

"And you have no doubt whatever that the man you saw is the prisoner?"

I couldn't make out what he was at. He couldn't have expected any other answer than the one he got.

"None whatever, sir. It isn't a face one forgets."

Counsel took a look round the court for a moment Then he said, "Do you mind, Mrs Salmon, examining again the people in court? No, not the prisoner. Stand up, please, Mr Adams," and there at the back of the court with thick stout body and muscular legs and a pair of bulging eyes, was the exact image of the man in the dock. He was even dressed the same – tight blue suit and striped tie.

"Now think very carefully, Mrs Salmon. Can you still swear that the man you saw drop the hammer in Mrs Parker's garden was the prisoner – and not this man who is his twin brother?"

Of course she couldn't. She looked from one to the other and didn't say a word.

There the big brute sat in the dock with his legs crossed and there he stood too at the back of the court and they both stared at Mrs Salmon. She shook her head.

What we saw then was the end of the case. There wasn't a witness prepared to swear that it was the prisoner he'd seen. And the brother? He had his alibi too; he was with his wife.

And so the man was acquitted for lack of evidence. But whether – if he did the murder and not his brother – he was punished or not, I don't know. That extraordinary

111

day had an extraordinary end. I followed Mrs Salmon out of court and we got wedged in the crowd who were waiting, of course, for the twins. The police tried to draw the crowd away, but all they could do was keep the road way clear for traffic. I learned later that they tried to get the twins to leave by a back way, but they wouldn't. One of them – no one knew which – said, "I've been acquitted, haven't I?" and they walked bang out of the front entrance. Then it happened. I don't know how, though I was only six feet away. The crowd moved and somehow one of the twins got pushed on the road right in front of a bus.

He gave a squeal like a rabbit and that was all; he was dead, his skull smashed just as Mrs Parker's had been. Divine vengeance? I wish I knew. There was the other Adams getting on his feet from beside the body and looking straight over at Mrs Salmon. He was crying, but whether he was the murderer or the innocent man nobody will ever be able to tell. But if you were Mrs Salmon, could you sleep at night?

The Killers

by Ernest Hemingway

A small American town; and in it a small "lunch-room" — what we'd call a cafe where you buy your food at the counter. It's called "Henry's", but a man called George runs it. Nick Adams is the only customer, until . . . the strangers come in.

The door of Henry's lunch-room opened and two men came in. They sat down at the counter.

"What's yours?" George asked them.

"I don't know," one of the men said. "What do you want to eat, Al?",

"I don't know," said Al. "I don't know what I want to eat."

Outside it was getting dark. The street light came on outside the window. The two men at the counter read the menu. From the other end of the counter Nick Adams watched them. He had been talking to George when they came in.

"I'll have a roast pork tenderloin with apple sauce and mashed potatoes," the first man said.

"It isn't ready yet."

"What the hell do you put it on the card for?"

"That's the dinner," George explained. "You can get that at six o'clock."

George looked at the clock on the wall behind the counter.

"It's five o'clock."

"The clock says twenty minutes past five," the second man said.

"It's twenty minutes fast."

"Oh, to hell with the clock," the first man said. "What have you got to eat?"

"I can give you any kind of sandwiches," George said. "You can have ham and eggs, bacon and eggs, liver and bacon, or a steak."

"Give me chicken croquettes with green peas and cream sauce and mashed potatoes."

"That's the dinner."

"Everything we want's the dinner, eh? That's the way you work it."

"I can give you ham and eggs, bacon and eggs, liver – "

"I'll take ham and eggs," the man called Al said. He wore a derby hat and a black overcoat buttoned across the chest. His face was small and white and he had tight lips. He wore a silk muffler and gloves.

"Give me bacon and eggs," said the other man. He was about the same size as Al. Their faces were different, but they were dressed like twins. Both wore overcoats too tight for them. They sat leaning forward, their elbows on the counter.

"Got anything to drink?" Al asked.

"Silver beer, bevo, ginger-ale," George said.

"I mean you got anything to *drink*?"

"Just those I said."

"This is a hot town," said the other. "What do they call it?"

"Summit."

"Ever hear of it?" Al asked his friend.

"No," said the friend.

"What do you do here nights?" Al asked.

"They eat the dinner," his friend said "They all come here and eat the big dinner."

"That's right," George said.

"So you think that's right?" Al asked George.

"Sure."

"You're a pretty bright boy, aren't you?"

"Sure," said George.

"Well, you're not," said the other little man. "Is he, Al?"

"He's dumb," said Al. He turned to Nick. "What's your name?"

"Adams."

"Another bright boy," Al said. "Ain't he a bright boy, Max?"

"The town's full of bright boys," Max said.

George put down two platters, one of ham and eggs, the other of bacon and eggs, on the counter. He set down two side dishes of fried potatoes and closed the wicket[1] into the kitchen.

"Which is yours?" he asked Al.

"Don't you remember?"

"Ham and eggs."

"Just a bright boy," Max said. He leaned forward and took the ham and eggs. Both men ate with their gloves on. George watched them eat.

1 *wicket*: a half-door.

"What are *you* looking at?" Max looked at George.

"Nothing."

"The hell you were. You were looking at me."

"Maybe the boy meant it for a joke Max," Al said.

George laughed.

"*You* don't have to laugh," Max said to him. "*You* don't have to laugh at all, see?"

"All right," said George.

"So he thinks it's all right," Max turned to Al. "He thinks it's all right. That's a good one."

"Oh, he's a thinker," Al said. They went on eating.

"What's the bright boy's name down the counter?" Al asked Max.

"Hey, bright boy," Max said to Nick. "You go around on the other side of the counter with your boy friend."

"What's the idea?" Nick asked.

"There isn't any idea."

"You better go around, bright boy," Al said. Nick went around behind the counter.

"What's the idea?" George asked.

"None of your damn business," Al said. "Who's out in the kitchen?"

"The nigger."

"What do you mean the nigger?"

"The nigger that cooks."

"Tell him to come in."

"What's the idea?"

"Tell him to come in."

"Where do you think you are?"

"We know damn well where we are," the man called Max said. "Do we look silly?"

"You talk silly," Al said to him. "What the hell do you argue with this kid for? Listen," he said to George, "tell the nigger to come out here."

"What are you going to do to him?"

"Nothing. Use your head, bright boy. What would we do to a nigger?"

George opened the slip that opened back into the kitchen "Sam," he called. "Come in here a minute."

The door of the kitchen opened and the nigger came in. "What was it?" he asked. The two men at the counter took a look at him.

"All right, nigger. You stand right there," Al said.

Sam, the nigger, standing in his apron, looked at the two men sitting at the counter. "Yes, sir," he said. Al got down from his stool.

"I'm going back to the kitchen with the nigger and bright boy," he said. "Go back to the kitchen, nigger. You go with him, bright boy." The little man walked after Nick and Sam, the cook, back into the kitchen. The door shut after them. The man called Max sat at the counter opposite George. He didn't look at George but looked in the mirror that ran along back of the counter. Henry's had been made over from a saloon into a lunch-counter.

'Well, bright boy," Max said, looking into the mirror, "why don't you say something?"

"What's it all about?"

"Hey, Al," Max called, "bright boy wants to know what it's all about."

"Why don't you tell him?" Al's voice came from the kitchen.

"What do you think it's all about?"

"I don't know."

"What do you think?"

Max looked into the mirror all the time he was talking.

"I wouldn't say."

"Hey, Al, bright boy says he wouldn't say what he thinks it's all about."

"I can hear you, all right," Al said from the kitchen. He had propped open the slit that dishes passed through into the kitchen with a catsup[1] bottle. "Listen, bright boy," he said from the kitchen to George. "Stand a little further along the bar. You move a little to the left, Max." He was like a photographer arranging for a group picture.

"Talk to me, bright boy," Max said. "What do you think's going to happen?"

George did not say anything.

"I'll tell you," Max said. "We're going to kill a Swede.

1 *catsup*: tomato sauce.

Do you know a big Swede named Ole Andreson?"

"Yes."

"He comes in here to eat every night, don't he?"

"Sometimes he comes here."

"He comes here at six o'clock, don't he?"

"If he comes."

"We know all that, bright boy," Max said. "Talk about something else. Ever go to the movies?"

"Once in a while."

"You ought to go to the movies more. The movies are fine for a bright boy like you."

"What are you going to kill Ole Andreson for? What did he ever do to you?"

"He never had a chance to do anything to us. He never even seen us."

"And he's only going to see us once," Al said from the kitchen.

"What are you going to kill him for, then?" George asked.

"We're killing him for a friend. Just to oblige a friend, bright boy."

"Shut up," said Al from the kitchen. "You talk too goddam much."

"Well, I got to keep bright boy amused. Don't I, bright boy?"

"You talk too damn much," Al said. "The nigger and my bright boy are amused by themselves. I got them tied up like a couple of girl friends in the convent."

"I suppose you were in a convent."

"You never know."

"You were in a kosher convent. That's where you were."

George looked up at the clock.

"If anybody comes in you tell them the cook is off, and if they keep after it, you tell them you'll go back and cook yourself. Do you get that, bright boy?"

"All right," George said. "What you going to do with us afterwards?"

"That'll depend," Max said. "That's one of those things you never know at the time."

George looked up at the clock. It was a quarter past

six. The door from the street opened. A street-car motor-man came in.

"Hello, George," he said. "Can I get supper?"

"Sam's gone out," George said. "He'll be back in about half-an-hour."

"I'd better go up the street," the motorman said. George looked at the clock. It was twenty minutes past six.

"That was nice, bright boy," Max said. "You're a regular little gentleman."

"He knew I'd blow his head off," Al said from the kitchen.

"No," said Max. "It ain't that. Bright boy is nice. He's a nice boy. I like him."

At six-fifty-five George said: "He's not coming."

Two other people had been in the lunch-room. Once George had gone out to the kitchen and made a ham-and-egg sandwich "to go" that a man wanted to take with him. Inside the kitchen he saw Al, his derby hat tilted back, sitting on a stool beside the wicket with the muzzle of a sawed-off shotgun resting on the ledge. Nick and the cook were back to back in the corner, a towel tied in each of their mouths George had cooked the sandwich, wrapped it up in oiled paper, put it in a bag, brought it in, and the man had paid for it and gone out.

"Bright boy can do everything," Max said. "He can cook and everything. You'd make some girl a nice wife, bright boy."

"Yes?" George said. "Your friend, Ole Andreson, isn't going to come."

"We'll give him ten minutes," Max said.

Max watched the mirror and the clock. The hands of the clock marked seven o'clock, and then five minutes past seven.

"Come on, Al," said Max. "We better go. He's not coming."

"Better give him five minutes," Al said from the kitchen.

In the five minutes a man came in, and George explained that the cook was sick.

"Why the hell don't you get another cook?" the man

asked. "Aren't you running a lunch-counter?" He went out.

"Come on, Al," Max said.

"What about the two bright boys and the nigger?"

"They're all right."

"You think so?"

"Sure. We're through with it."

"I don't like it," said Al. "It's sloppy. You talk too much."

"Oh, what the hell," said Max. "We got to keep amused, haven't we?"

"You talk too much, all the same," Al said. He came out from the kitchen. The cut-off barrels of the shotgun made a slight bulge under the waist of his too tight-fitting overcoat. He straightened his coat with his gloved hands.

"So long, bright boy," he said to George. "You got a lot of luck."

"That's the truth," Max said. "You ought to play the races, bright boy."

The two of them went out of the door. George watched them, through the window, pass under the arc-light and cross the street. In their tight overcoats and derby hats they looked like a vaudeville team. George went back through the swinging-door into the kitchen and untied Nick and the cook.

"I don't want any more of that," said Sam, the cook. "I don't want any more of that."

Nick stood up. He had never had a towel in his mouth before.

"Say," he said. "What the hell?" He was trying to swagger it off.

"They were going to kill Ole Andreson," George said. "They were going to shoot him when he came in to eat."

"Ole Andreson?"

"Sure."

The cook felt the corners of his mouth with his thumbs.

"They all gone?" he asked.

"Yeah," said George. "They're gone now."

"I don't like it," said the cook. "I don't like any of it at all."

"Listen," George said to Nick. "You better go see Ole Andreson."

"All right."

"You better not have anything to do with it at all," Sam, the cook, said. "You better stay way out of it."

"Don't go if you don't want to," George said.

"Mixing up in this ain't going to get you anywhere," the cook said. "You stay out of it."

"I'll go see him," Nick said to George. "Where does he live?"

The cook turned away.

"Little boys always know what they want to do," he said.

"He lives up at Hirsch's rooming-house," George said to Nick.

"I'll go up there."

Outside, the arc light shone through the bare branches of a tree. Nick walked up the street beside the car-tracks and turned at the next arc light down a side-street. Three houses up the street was Hirsch's rooming-house. Nick walked up the two steps and pushed the bell. A woman came to the door.

"Is Ole Andreson here?"

"Do you want to see him?"

"Yes, if he's in."

Nick followed the woman up a flight of stairs and back to the end of the corridor. She knocked on the door.

"Who is it?"

"It's somebody to see you, Mr Andreson," the woman said.

"It's Nick Adams."

"Come in."

Nick opened the door and went into the room. Ole Andreson was lying on the bed with all his clothes on. He had been a heavyweight prize-fighter and he was too long for the bed. He lay with his head on two pillows. He did not look at Nick.

"What was it?" he asked.

"I was up at Henry's," Nick said, "and two fellows came in and tied up me and the cook, and they said they were going to kill you."

It sounded silly when he said it. Ole Andreson said nothing.

"They put us out in the kitchen," Nick went on. "They were going to shoot you when you came in to supper."

Ole Andreson looked at the wall and did not say anything.

"George thought I'd better come and tell you about."

"There isn't anything I can do about it," Ole Andreson said.

"I'll tell you what they were like."

"I don't want to know what they were like," Ole Andreson said. He looked at the wall. "Thanks for coming to tell me about it."

"That's all right."

Nick looked at the big man lying on the bed.

"Don't you want me to go and see the police?"

"No," Ole Andreson said. "That wouldn't do any good."

"Isn't there something I could do?"

"No. There ain't anything to do."

"Maybe it was just a bluff."

"No. It ain't just a bluff."

Ole Andreson rolled over towards the wall.

"The only thing is," he said, talking towards the wall, "I just can't make up my mind to go out. I been in here all day."

"Couldn't you get out of town?"

"No," Ole Andreson said. "I'm through with all that running around."

He looked at the wall.

"There ain't anything to do now."

"Couldn't you fix it up some way?"

"No. I got in wrong." He talked in the same flat voice. "There ain't anything to do. After a while I'll make up my mind to go out."

"I better go back and see George," Nick said.

"So long," said Ole Andreson. He did not look towards Nick. "Thanks for coming around."

Nick went out. As he shut the door he saw Ole Andreson with all his clothes on, lying on the bed looking at the wall.

"He's been in his room all day," the landlady said downstairs. "I guess he don't feel well. I said to him: 'Mr Andreson, you ought to go out and take a walk on a nice fall[1] day like this,' but he didn't feel like it."

"He doesn't want to go out."

"I'm sorry he don't feel well," the woman said. "He's an awfully nice man. He was in the ring, you know."

"I know it."

"You'd never know it except from the way his face is," the woman said. They stood talking just inside the street door. "He's just as gentle."

"Well, goodnight, Mrs Hirsch," Nick said.

"I'm not Mrs Hirsch," the woman said. "She owns the place. I just look after it for her. I'm Mrs Bell."

"Well, goodnight, Mrs Bell," Nick said.

"Good-night," the woman said.

Nick walked up the dark street to the corner under the arc light, and then along the car-tracks to Henry's eating-house. George was inside, back of the counter.

"Did you see Ole?"

"Yes," said Nick. "He's in his room and he won't go out."

The cook opened the door from the kitchen when he heard Nick's voice.

"I don't even listen to it," he said and shut the door.

"Did you tell him about it?" George asked.

"Sure. I told him, but he knows what it's all about."

"What's he going to do?"

"Nothing."

"They'll kill him."

"I guess they will."

"He must have got mixed up in something in Chicago."

"I guess so," said Nick.

"It's a hell of a thing."

"It's an awful thing," Nick said.

They did not say anything. George reached down for a towel and wiped the counter.

1 *fall*: autumn.

"I wonder what he did?" Nick said.

"Double-crossed somebody. That's what they kill them for."

"I'm going to get out of this town," Nick said.

"Yes," said George. "That's a good thing to do."

"I can't stand to think about him waiting in the room and knowing he's going to get it. It's too damned awful."

"Well," said George, "you better not think about it."

Hallmarked
by Walter Macken

A precious gold or silver object is given a mark by the craftsman who has manufactured it. This makes it clear to everyone who comes across it in the future exactly where it was made and what it is worth. This sign is called a "hall mark". The object is marked for ever, and easy to recognise.

This story takes us to a very remote part of Ireland, a tiny country village to which strangers almost never come. In it we go to the village shop, run by Michael John.

Michael John sold everything.

He could see you in and see you out of the world, simple or de luxe, at both ends at a fair price and no middlemen. While you were in it he could sustain you with food or drink for man, child or beast, of any sex, creed or generation. He could post a letter for you that would go several times around the world if you wanted, or by speaking at the bit of wire he could let you talk to His Holiness the Pope in Rome if the man wasn't too busy to have a chat with you.

It was the only shop in the village and it sold everything. Strangers rarely found their way into it. It was in the middle of the mountains down a glen that bore a river that was running mad for the sea. It was a long bad road that led into it from the main road, too rocky and potholed for posh cars, too hilly for bicycles, too uninviting for shanks's mare. Everyone in it was quite happy as far as happiness goes, and they didn't care if they never saw a stranger. But if one came they could put up with him and tell him what was happening where he came from because they were great people for knowing everything, having wireless sets and weekly papers and legions of relations in America who sent them big bundles of glossy magazines and hair-raising comics that they read themselves but kept away from the children because most of the lassies in the pictures were more than half naked and were showing more of their bumps to the world than a rawhide cow, bless the mark.

So Michael John was a little surprised one fine spring morning, looking out his small windowpane while he was rubbing a pint glass, to see a stranger coming out of the crutch of the hill and walking down the main road. He was a tall man dressed in a dark suit. The boots he was wearing and the bottoms of his trousers were covered in dust. He's come far, Michael John thought wisely, and he walked it. There was a great breadth of shoulder on him and he had very long arms hanging straight down. They were almost below his knees. His head was bare and his short hair was very grey and there was a sort of yellow look about his face. He paused in the middle of the road. There were only four houses to be seen. The other few were hidden over the shoulder of the hills. He saw the nearly obliterated sign about licence to sell tobacco outside Michael John's and he headed that way. Michael John pulled away from the window. The shop was part of the house. He had a small piece of a counter and the big open fire was blazing, because even though it was a spring day there was snow on the top of the hills and you would be frozen if you weren't working. A few barrels and a few chairs and all the rest shelves holding his goods. You'd wonder how in the name of God he knew where to lay his hands on things, but he did.

The man darkened the door.

"Good day," said Michael John.

The man came in. He could see his face. All expression seemed to be wiped out of it. A big face, with bulging muscles on the jaws and a strong nose. Calm brown eyes that seemed to have no expression in them either. Michael John liked the man from the look of him. That was the way he was. He would like you or not. If he liked you and you turned out bad he would always find excuses for you. If he didn't like you and you turned out to be a saint he would question the choir of angels that worked the miracles in your name.

"It's a nice day," said the man. His voice seemed to be rusty.

"It is, thank God," said Michael John.

"Thank God again," said the man. "I'd like to buy a loaf of bread and a little cheese and a bottle of stout," he said.

"It's a pleasure," said Michael John, reaching for them.

"Would it offend you if I eat them here?" the man asked.

"It would not," said Michael John. He thought the man had good manners anyhow.

He watched the man eating. He ate slowly and carefully. He chewed every bit of the bread and cheese slowly and washed it down his throat with the stout. He took a purse out of his pocket then and he extracted a few coins and he paid, and Michael John thought he was old-fashioned. Very few men carried the little leather purses nowadays. He wasn't as young as he had looked walking to the house. Michael John thought he would be more than fifty. But well set up still. Muscles were bulging his coat sleeves. He had no spare flesh on him. Michael John was puzzled by him.

He cut tobacco and filled a pipe and lighted it. Then he looked at Michael John.

"This is a nice spot," he said. "Is it lonely?"

"I don't know," said Michael John. "We like it. Is it lonely? I don't know. We haven't time to be lonely."

"I don't mean that way," said the man. "I mean many strangers don't find their way into it."

"We're rarely troubled," said Michael John.

"When I came in by the fork on the hills," said the man, "I saw a green space up in the middle of the heather. There is a house there too with a latch on it. Like it was a small farm carved out of the hills that was left to lie."

"That's right," said Michael John. "That's a place."

"Does it belong to people?" he asked.

"It belongs to me," said Michael John. "I was born in that house. Me grandfather died in it. We couldn't shift him down here."

That paused the man. His big hands rubbed against each other.

"Would you let me live there?" he asked. Out. Direct. Michael John was nonplussed.

"It's not in good shape," he said. "The thatch is bad. It must be leaking inside. There'd want to be an awful lot done to it."

"I'll do it," said the man. "I'll do all that wants to be done to it, and I'll clear the fields of the ferns and the gorse that's grown up in it. I'll make it very tidy for you and I'll pay you within my means."

"It's a long way from company," said Michael John. "In the bad winter there's no way out of it. A person'd be snowed up like the sheep."

"I'd like it that way," said the man.

"Where are you from?" Michael John asked.

"I'd like not to tell you that," the man said earnestly. "I'd just like to fix that little house and let me go in there and no sinner know about me. I could tell you I'm from here or there but I don't want to tell you. Just that if you think I'm honest you will oblige me, and if you don't think so just let it lie."

Michael John thought. He looked into the brown eyes that were calmly fixed on his own. Michael John had a big, cheerful, ugly face that was very readable. The man knew he had succeeded when he saw the crinkling eyes.

"All right," said Michael John.

A soft sigh escaped from the man. Michael John was surprised. A terrible lot depended on that, he thought.

"My name is Paul," said the man.

"Shake on it so, Paul," said Michael John, holding out his hand.

Paul seemed to hesitate, and then put out his hand. It was as hard as rock, Michael John felt.

"You do it up, and when you have it fixed we can talk about a payment from then," said Michael John. "Up to that it will be like you are working for me."

The man looked his thanks. For one of the few times in his life Michael John was embarrassed at the gratitude looking out of the man's eyes. That look should only be in the eyes of a sick dog, he thought.

If the people wanted something to talk about they had it now. They wanted to know everything. Michael John, knowing very little more than themselves, had to pretend to be very mysterious. That went well. Just a friend of mine, said Michael John, from the other side of the country. Bad health. Building himself up.

In three months you wouldn't know the small place on the side of the hill. From being sad and decayed and green-moulded the house became yellow and white and glittering. The man never seemed to stop working. Under a spade the hard little fields groaned off their green and the cleared rocks became neat stone walls all around them. It was like a miracle on the side of a hill. The fairies couldn't have done better. But nobody could get close to the fellow. He would return your greeting and agree about the weather and drink a bottle with you in Michael John's in the calm of the evening. But that's all. His name was Paul. He had lost his yellow look. He was brown and strong and one of the hardest-working men they had ever met. And one of the happiest. The contentment that flowed out of the man was even enough to kill your curiosity. They became fond of him, and proud of his place, and Michael John became possessive about him, as if he had got him from Santa Claus for Christmas.

The inside of the house was good. The furniture he made himself wasn't crude. It was smooth and well made and solid like himself. The kids liked him. Apparently they understood his silence. He could make the queerest yokes with a knife that you ever saw out of bits of bogdeal or the roots of briars. There wasn't a kid in the place that didn't have one of them. The parents often questioned the children about him. What did he say? (Arrah, nothin'.) What did he do? (Arrah, nothin'.) Eventually they gave up probing and just accepted him.

Until the motor car made its way into the mountains the following spring.

If you stood on the top of the hills and looked down at it you would be appalled at the terrible struggle it was having. It jolted and bumped and swayed, and steam came from under it like a monster. It wasn't the only car that had come in there. Lorries had come before and often did bring supplies in to Michael John. But lorry drivers are very reckless people and would drive a lorry in and out of hell as long as they didn't own it themselves.

Paul was working at the roadway he was making into the place. It was a cruel hard job, but he had conquered the boggy bits and the granite bits and it was a pleasant path to look at running up and hugging the contours of the hillside. He saw the car making its way and he leaned on the spade to watch it come. If he had seen it a year ago coming it might have given him uneasiness, but he was a different man now. There was nothing before him but his life. He had buried the years that were gone in his sweat.

The man driving the car was small and tubby. He could no longer see his crotch for his stomach. He had rimless glasses and his face was a round blob that was decorated with a small nose and a small mouth and small eyes. He travelled for people. He sold all sorts of things for them. He was very successful because he often did what he was doing now, following the bad byroads that other men would have thought too much trouble.

As the steaming, groaning car came closer Paul pretended to be working away. But he couldn't kill the curiosity and looked back now and again over his shoulder. The car stopped below him with a lurch. The window rolled down. He heard the small high voice calling him. He turned and ambled down to stand beside the car. He could feel the heat from it. Then he saw the face of the little man and his life was destroyed. The man tried to cover the recognition in his face, but it was too late. Paul had seen it. Bitterness flooded over him and a black despair. His hands tightened on the spade. The man was frightened when he saw the white beside his nostrils. Then Paul turned away and went trudging up the hill. The little fat fellow called after him, to cover up.

"Hi, mister, is this the way in to Michael John's?"

The man, didn't turn back to answer him. He kept striding up the hill.

He let in the clutch and went on.

He was gleeful. Who'd ever believe? He heard himself telling the story in the commercial room of every tuppenny-hapenny hotel in the country. The twist and the build-up and the climax. Did these people in here know? What do you bet they didn't know? I bet you a fiver they don't know. Wait'll they hear. Man, who'd have thought in the middle of a wilderness like this? He went down into the valley at speed. He didn't notice the tumbling river, the glittering sea in the distance, the sun shining brightly on the white-faced cottages, the heather of the hills throwing off the frost, the sedge shooting green shoots. He saw nothing because he was really only a little blind man who thought about nothing except commission and dirty stories.

Michael John was in the shop, and two more of the men. He didn't try to sell anything even. He started straight off.

"Hey! How are ye, men? I met a fella up on the side of the hill. Know who he was?"

"That's Paul," said Michael John.

"Paul, my Aunt Fanny!" said the little fat fellow. "That's James Brian that killed his wife twelve years ago, down in the town. Came home drunk he did and didn't know his own strength. Listen, man. Listen to the cream of it. Know who was foreman of the jury that convicted him? Me! Imagine that? Did you ever hear the like of that?"

"Listen," said Michael John tensely. "Did you talk to him?"

"No fear," said the little fellow. "Not me. Talk to a murderer, is it? He took one look at me and he went up the hill as if the devil was after him."

Michael John left the shop at a run. He was cursing and cursing. He wasn't built for running any more. He was slow in the legs and heavy around the waist but he ran. Up the road and around towards the curve of the hill, holding his hand at his chest to stop his heart from bursting. His tongue was hanging out on his cheek like a pointer dog in the heather.

And he was too late. That was what he was afraid of.

He stood there and called to the small figure down in the valley. The small figure of the big man leaping down. He had the suit on that he came with and nothing at all in his hands or in his pockets or on his back. He was going out the very same way he came in. Michael John stood there and called: "Paul! Paul!" He called and the hills carried his call away and over the man and threw it off the hills and sent it back to him. He saw the figure of the man stand as if he had been hit with a bullet, hesitate and then run on. Michael John shouted "Paul!" once more, but it was no use, and he knew it was no use. Tears of anger and sadness came into his eyes and he had to bend in two coughing from the way the breath was strangling in him from the unaccustomed running. And then when the spasm was finished he turned and walked back to the group at the door of the shop.

The little fat one saw him looking at him with red-rimmed eyes.

"Get out of here, you little bastard," said Michael John. "And if you put a foot in this place again I'll shoot you."

"Now look here," said the little fellow with the bounce he used to sell people things they didn't want.

"Get out of here," Michael John roared at him, scrabbling at his shoulder and pushing him towards his car. "Get out of here while you have unlet blood in you, you ball of filth, before I cripple you."

"But – " said the fellow, and then after a look at Michael John's face he leaped into the car and shot away. Michael John bent and took up a rock from the road and flung it at the car. It bounced off the black paint, leaving a dint in it.

Then the anger left his face. His clenched hands unloosed themselves.

He walked into the shop. He went over towards the fire. He sat on a stool there and he lowered his face into his hands.

Twenty Pieces of Silver

by Stan Barstow

Some years ago Mrs Fosdyke was tempted to steal. She is an elderly woman now, and her husband is dead. She unexpectedly tells all about the temptation to two visitors – two sisters called Miss Norris, who are better off than Mrs Fosdyke, and who help organise local charities. When they call on Mrs Fosdyke, they find her dressed in black as she has been to a funeral.

When the Misses Norris, in pursuance of their good works, called on little Mrs Fosdyke at her tiny terrace house in Parker Street she answered their discreet knock dressed for going out. They apologised then in their quiet, genteel way and said they would call again. But Mrs Fosdyke beckoned them into the house. "I've just come in," she said. "A minute or two earlier and you'd have followed me down the street." It was then that the Misses Norris realised that Mrs Fosdyke was dressed in black, the hat shop-bought but the coat probably run up on her own machine, and, as if reading their minds, she said, "I've just been to a funeral," and the Misses Norris murmured "Oh?" for no one of their acquaintance had died during the past week.

They sat down when asked to, the elder Miss Norris on the edge of the armchair by the table, legs tucked neatly away behind her skirt; the younger Miss Norris upright on a chair by the window. Mrs Fosdyke slipped off her coat and occupied herself with kettle and teapot at the sink in the corner.

"You'll have a cup o' tea?" she asked, the spoon with the second measure poised over the pot.

"Well..." the younger Miss Norris began, and her sister said, with the poise and grace of her extra years, "You're very kind."

"I hate funerals," Mrs Fosdyke said converstionally as she poured boiling water into the pot. "If it's anybody you thought anything of they upset you; and if it's somebody you didn't like you feel a hypocrite."

She took two more cups and saucers from the cupboard over the sink, wiping them thoroughly on the teatowel before setting them out alongside her own on the oilcloth-covered top of the clothes-wringer under the window.

"Was it a relative?" the younger Miss Norris ventured.

Mrs Fosdyke shook her head. "No, a friend. A good friend. Mrs Marsden from up Hilltop. Don't know if you knew her. A widow, like me. Her husband died five or six years back. He used to be something in textiles over Bradford way. Quite well-to-do, they were. Poor dear...

She had cancer, y'know. It was a happy release for her."

She poured the tea, handing the Misses Norris a cup each and passing the sugar bowl and milk jug to each in turn. She herself remained standing, between the wringer and the sink, the late-morning sun lighting her grey hair below the little black hat.

"Funny," the said reflectively, between sips. "Fifteen years I'd known Mrs Marsden, and it might only have been a month or two. Funny how friendships start...

"I answered an advertisement in the *Argus*, y'know. That's how I came to go in the first place. Jim was alive then and he'd just taken to his wheelchair. I was looking for work but I couldn't take on a full-time job because of having him to see to. So I got a few cleaning jobs that kept me busy six mornings a week. Mrs Marsden's was one of them. Three mornings, I went to her.

"I didn't think I was going to stick it at first. There was nothing wrong with the job or the money, mind; but they hadn't started running buses up to Hilltop at that time, and it was a mile and a half uphill from town. A rare drag, it was, and it seemed to get longer and steeper and harder every morning I went there. Anyway, I needed the money, and that was that.

"I knew when Jim first went down it wouldn't be easy, but I told meself we'd manage. Just so long as I could keep going."

+The Misses Norris, neither of whom had ever done anything more strenuous about a house than vacuum a carpet, murmured in sympathy and understanding and sipped their tea.

"Well, it wasn't too bad when I'd got used to it – the going out and cleaning, I mean. We managed. Mrs Reed next door kept her eye on Jim in the mornings, and I did my own cleaning and my shopping in the afternoons. We'd always been ones for simple pleasures. We liked the chapel. There were the services on Sundays and the Women's Bright Hour on Wednesday afternoons, and I used to park Jim's chair in the porch where he could hear the singing and watch what was going on in the street. And then there were the Saturday night concerts in the schoolroom – though they don't have so many of them nowadays – and anybody who was willing did a turn. I can see Jim's face now, all flushed and cheerful, his head nodding to the music..."

"He was a brave and cheerful man, Mrs Fosdyke," said the elder Miss Norris. "We all admired his courage."

"Aye, aye. Well, of course, you know all about the chapel and the Bright Hour, an' that.

"Well, Mrs Marsden made me realise you could be well off and still unhappy. That you could be lacking in peace and quietness of mind even with no money worries, and a husband in good health.

"I remember the first time we talked as woman to woman. It came up because it was a Wednesday and I wanted to finish prompt on twelve so's I could get done at home in time for the Bright Hour. It was my first week with Mrs Marsden and I had to explain the position.

" 'I don't mind stopping a bit extra on Mondays and Fridays, if you need me,' I said, 'but I shouldn't like to miss my Bright Hour on a Wednesday.'

" 'I'm sure I shouldn't like to be the one to keep you away,' she said, and there was something a bit odd in her voice that puzzled me. But nothing more was said till the Wednesday after, and then she brought it up herself, and this queer something in her voice was there again, and I asked her if she didn't go to a place of worship herself, then.

" 'I used to,' she said, 'a long time ago. I was brought up in the Church. I was on several committees. I worked like a slave for it.'

" 'And whatever made you give it up, then?' I said.

" 'I lost all reason for going,' she said.

"I was a bit shocked then. 'You mean,' I said, 'you lost your faith in God?'

"As soon as I'd said it, of course, I was sorry I'd pried. It was none of my business, after all.

"And then, after a minute, she said 'Yes.' Just like that: straight out.

"I remember clearly as if it were yesterday, knocking off the vacuum-cleaner and looking at her. I knew lots of people who never went to either chapel or church, but I'd never come face to face with one who said straight out she was atheist. Because, that's what it amounted to.

"So I said to her, 'Well, I mean, it's none of my business, but what ever did that to you?'

"And she rolled her duster up and her face went all hard. 'I had a boy,' she said. 'He died.'

"I could feel for her. 'That's terrible,' I said. 'But lots of people –'

"'But this was *my* boy,' she said.. 'For ten years we prayed for a child. We prayed and prayed, and then eventually he came. He was an imbecile. He died when he was three. Have you ever had an idiot child, Mrs Fosdyke?' she said, and she was so twisted up with bitterness inside her I could hardly bear to look at her..

"So I said, no, I hadn't. 'But I've seen a fine God-fearing man struck down in his prime and condemned to spend the rest of his days in a wheelchair,' I said. 'I can sympathise with you, Mrs Marsden.'

"'And yet you still believe,' she said, and she was full of impatience and anger. 'How can you believe in a God of love who allows these things?'

"'Wouldn't it be easy to believe if everything in the world was fine and grand?' I said. 'Anybody could believe with no trouble at all. But that's not God's way. He has to send suffering to try us, to steel us and purify us.'

"'Oh, stuff and nonsense,' she said. 'I've heard it all before. What does a little child know of these things?'

"'I know, I know,' I said. 'It's hard to understand. But how can he make an exception for children? There has to be danger for them, just like grown-ups.'

"So she just turned her back on me then and polished away at the dresser. And then she spun round on me in a second. 'But how can you reconcile yourself to it?' she said. 'How can you accept it?'

"'It's one of those things you can't argue out, Mrs Marsden,' I said. 'You can talk about it till Domesday and get no forrader. It's something you've got to feel. And I reckon you either feel it or you don't. How can I accept it, you say. Why, what else can I do? If I lose that, I've nothing else left.' And I looked at her and I said, 'But you do miss it, don't you, you poor dear?'

"I'd gone a bit too far there. She drew herself up and went all chilly. She was a very thin woman, you know, and she could look very proud when she set herself. 'I don't need your pity, thank you,' she said. 'What you believe is your own business...You can finish the carpet now,' she said, 'if you don't mind.'

"I was sorry afterwards that it had happened. I was beginning to find in this business of going into other women's homes that a friendly but respectful relationship was the best on both sides, and I didn't want to spoil anything...

"Another cup? Oh, go on; it'll just be wasted if you don't...That's right."

The two Misses Norris allowed their cups to be refilled, and since they had nothing else to do that morning which could not be done later, settled back in comfort to hear whatever else Mrs Fosdyke would tell them of her relationship with the late Mrs Marsden.

"She wouldn't leave it alone, though," Mrs Fosdyke said. "She seemed to be waiting for chances to bring it up again. She seemed to have to let out that sourness and bitterness inside her. I didn't like it, and I did think of leaving her. But I decided I could stand it. She wasn't a bad employer, and I needed the money. Pride has to take a bit of a back seat when you're in the position I was in then.

"Anyway, I'd been working for her for six months, and one Wednesday I went up there as usual. The mornings passed quickly, and it seemed like twelve o'clock came almost before I'd gotten started. As I was putting my things on to go, Mrs Marsden remembered two things at once. She wanted me to leave one of her husband's suits at the cleaners, and she had to nip out to see a neighbour who'd be going out at any minute.

"So she came into the kitchen with the suit draped all any-old-how over her arm. 'Here we are,' she said. 'He hasn't worn it for some time. I'd like to see if it will clean up decently. Now if I don't hurry I shall miss Mrs Wilson.

You'll find paper and string in that cupboard; and you might just go through the pockets before you wrap it up. I haven't time, myself.' And with a last reminder to drop the latch as I went out, she was off.

"I had a look at the suit then. It looked nearly new to me, and I thought to myself 'Fancy being able to cast aside a suit like this.' I hadn't got to the stage of begging clothes, but I was tempted at times. Jim had never had a suit like that in his life.

"Well, I took each part of it in turn and brushed it down with the flat of my hand and went through all the pockets. When I got to the waistcoat I more felt than heard something crackle in one of the pockets, and when I put my fingers in I pulled out a pound note, folded in two. So from thinking about Mr Marsden discarding good clothes I got to thinking about a 'carry on' that could allow a pound note to be lost without being missed.

"I popped it down on a corner of the kitchen cabinet and wrapped the suit in brown paper. I found myself glancing sideways at the note. Who knew about it but me? A pound...twenty shillings. What was a pound to the Marsdens? And what was a pound to Jim and me? There were few enough ever came our way, and every one was hard earned, every shilling to be held on to till I couldn't help spending it. Things had been tighter than usual lately, as well. We'd had a lot of expense. I took the note into my hand and thought of all it could buy. Fruit for Jim, and a bit of tobacco – always a special treat. And he needed new underclothes. And I'd planned to get him a bottle of the tonic wine that seemed to buck him up so.

"So I stood there in Mrs Marsden's kitchen with her husband's pound note screwed up in a little ball in my hand where nobody else could see it; and it was just as though there was nothing else in the world but that note and my need of it."

Mrs Fosdyke's voice had grown softer and now it died away altogether as she stopped speaking and gazed out through the window. The two sisters exchanged a swift glance before she stirred and turned to put her empty cup on the draining-board.

"Well, that was a Wednesday, like I said. And on the Friday I went up to the house again. I was there at nine, my usual time. I remember distinctly that it was a rainy morning. Not heavy rain, but that thin, fine stuff that seems to wet you through more thoroughly than an out-and-out downpour. Anyway, I was soaked by the time I got there, and when I'd changed into my working-shoes, I took my coat upstairs to let it drip into the bath. Then I helped Mrs Marsden with the few breakfast pots and we got going on the downstairs rooms, like we always did on a Friday.

"She was a bit quiet that morning, Mrs Marsden was, and I thought perhaps she wasn't feeling too well. At eleven we knocked off for five minutes and went into the kitchen for a cup of tea and a biscuit. And then Mrs Marsden said, just casual like, 'By the way,' she said, 'Mr Marsden seems to think he left some money in that suit you took to the cleaners. Did you find anything when you looked through the pockets?'

"I'd clean forgotten about it till she mentioned it. I put my cup down and got up and felt under one of the canisters on the shelf. 'You didn't see it, then?' I said. 'I popped it up there on Wednesday. I meant to mention it, but I get more forgetful every day. That's all there was: just the odd note.' I wondered she didn't notice the tremble in my fingers as I handed it to her.

"She spread the note out by her plate and said she'd give it to Mr Marsden when he came home. And I said it was funny that he'd bethought himself about it after all that time. I remembered she'd said he hadn't worn the suit for some while.

" 'Well,' she said, 'you see -er-er . . .' And she got all sort of tongue-tied, and then I knew there was something wrong somewhere. I didn't like the look on her face, for a start. And then it came over me, all at once.

" 'Why,' I said, 'I believe you put that money in your husband's suit. I don't think he knows anything about it. You put it there deliberately, hoping I'd take it and say nothing.'

"She went red then; her face coloured like fire. 'I have

141

to test the honesty of my servants,' she said, sort of proud like, but uneasy under it.

"And it got my rag out, that did. I was blazing mad. 'Well, you tested mine,' I said. 'And if it's any joy to you, I'll admit I was sorely tempted. Isn't it enough that you should lose your way without making me lose mine? A pound, Mrs Marsden,' I said. 'Twenty pieces of silver. Is that my price, d'you think? They gave Judas thirty!'[1]

"She got up. 'I don't have to take this kind of talk from you,' she said, and brushed past me and ran upstairs.

"I sat down at the table and put my head in my hands. I was near to tears. I couldn't understand it. I just couldn't understand what had made her do it. And I said a little prayer of thanks. 'O God,' I said, 'only You knew how near I was.'

"In a few minutes I got up and went and listened at the foot of the stairs. I went up to the bathroom and got my coat. I stood for a minute then. There was no place for me here in the future. I felt like leaving straight away: walking out without another word. But I was due to a week's wages and I couldn't afford pride of that sort.

"So I called out softly, 'Mrs Marsden.'

"But there was no reply. I went across the landing to her bedroom door and listened. I could hear something then, but I wasn't quite sure what it was. I called again, and when nobody answered I tapped on the door and went in. She was lying on one of the twin beds with her face to the window. I could tell now it was sobbing I'd heard and her shoulders shook as I stood and watched her. There was something about her that touched me right to the quick, and I put my coat down and went to her and put my hand on her shoulder. 'There, there,' I said, 'don't take on so. There's no harm done.' I sat down behind her on the bed, and all at once she put her hand up and took mine. 'Don't go away,' she said. 'Don't leave me now.'

"I remember just the feeling I had then. It was like a

---

1 Judas was the follower of Christ who betrayed him to earn himself "thirty pieces of silver"

great rush of joy: the sort of feeling you get when you know you're wanted, that somebody needs you.

"'Of course I won't leave you,' I said. 'Of course I won't.'"

Mrs Fosdyke sighed and turned from the window. "And I never did," she said. "I never did."

She looked at each of the sisters in turn. "Well," she said, a bashful little smile coming to her lips, "I've never told anybody about that before. But this morning sort of brought it all back. And she's gone beyond harm now, poor dear."

She glanced at the clock on the mantelpiece. "Gracious, look at the time! And me keeping you sat with my chatter."

"But what a lovely story," said the younger Miss Norris, who was of a romantic turn of mind. "It's like something out of the Bible."

"Well, that's as maybe," Mrs Fosdyke said briskly, "but I'm sure you didn't call to hear me tell the tale."

"As a matter of fact," the elder Miss Norris said, drawing a sheaf of papers from her large handbag, "we're organising the collection for the orphanage and we wondered if you could manage this district again this year. We know how busy you are."

"Well –" Mrs Fosdyke put her finger to her chin – "I suppose I *could* fit it in."

"You're such a *good* collector, Mrs Fosdyke," the younger Miss Norris said. "Everybody gives so generously when you go round."

"Aye, well, I suppose I can manage it," Mrs Fosdyke said, and the Misses Norris beamed at her.

"Oh, we know the willing hearts and hands, Mrs Fosdyke," the elder sister said.

"I suppose you do," said Mrs Fosdyke, with a hint of dryness in her voice.

"There'll be a place in heaven for you, Mrs Fosdyke," gushed the younger Miss Norris.

"Oh, go on with you," Mrs Fosdyke said. "Somebody's got to look out for the poor lambs, haven't they?"

The Ice Cream
by Elian Toona

*Jack is a young boy who has lost his parents, and is looked after
in a residential home. People who want to help call to visit the
boys to take them out once a month. Jack's "Aunty" is not getting
on very well with him. They both seem miserable. She's cross
and so is he. Who is at fault? She has bought him a treat – a very
large ice cream, but will he eat it?*

The table barely reached Jack's chin, but the ice cream towered above him. A small breeze was playing with the edges of the red-and-white check tablecloth and the tight smile on the corners of "Aunt's" mouth. The table was outside under the trees and it was raining pink blossoms all the time, which fell around the glass and were piling up on the ice cream unheeded.

It had suddenly turned warm. Warmer than would have been expected for this early time of year and the people were still in winter clothing. Many of them had now removed their overcoats and were carrying them over their arm. Some had stopped by benches and were sitting there with their upturned faces held towards the sun. Eyes closed.

The chairs and tables outside the pavement cafe were all occupied. Jack was sitting opposite his "Auntie". She too had her coat open showing her heavy tweed suit. Her eyes were closed, but they appeared to be pressed together in patience rather then pleasure. The smile still lingered, but probably because her hair was pulled back too tight, thought Jack, and the pain of it was causing that expression. Jack too was dressed for winter. Wearing the grey winter uniform which everyone around here recognised on sight. His shoes and stocking were like his "Aunt's", except that his were black and hers were brown. Auntie's legs seemed to be growing out of felt, with pink blossoms crawling in among the laces.

The aunt rearranged herself. Mainly to shift the handbag in her lap. She opened her eyes for a moment and shot a quick piercing glance across the table. Hmm! Jack hadn't moved. He was still hiding behind the ice cream, clutching the spoon like a sword as long as his arm.

The avenue was lined by flowering chestnuts and the pavement was almost as wide as the main road, but still it was completely covered by branches. The sun shone in rays through the lace and picked out certain objects: the glasses that sparkled with different colours, car mirrors from the main road, chrome that shone like silver. There were birds up in the trees and birds under the tables, getting into everybody's way. But Jack didn't seem to be aware of anything. He was looking at the table, at his school cap which was lying next to "Auntie's" newspaper. The cap had a blue band around it which proclaimed to everyone that he belonged to the *HOME*. The big well-known home which had a wall seven foot high with glass on top of it – glass pressed in cement, like wafers into ice cream. Ice cream! He looked at the one on the table, at this super giant ice cream, the same kind he had always wanted and dreamt about, all his life! With strawberries, chocolate sauce, whitish yellow cream, nuts and those two wafers, like ears. And that glass made him dizzy with its facets of colours. But he made no move towards it.

"Auntie" opened her eyes once more. Changing tactics, she spread her stawberry coloured lips wide across the whitish-yellow cream teeth. "Eat, child. Eat," she coaxed. But Jack was following her eyes, which were not smiling.

People passed close to their table. All the other tables were taken and voices mingled with traffic noises. Spoons clattered against glass, cups against saucers. Spirits were high and abandoned after the long winter. Many who passed looked twice at the woman and child. Not only because they knew it was the last Sunday in the month. That today was the Sunday when "visiting Aunts" called at the Home to bring out their charges all in the name of charity. But because the two seemed like statues, void of contact and yet tied together. So long already, that the ice cream had started to melt.

Jack opened his mouth. He was going to say something. But he didn't. No one understood the way his words got tied in his throat. He swallowed hard and dropped his gaze under the table. Aunt's fingers were nervously picking at the clasp of her handbag.

"Well, I never!" thought Auntie, at first, with righteous indignation but as time passed she began to see it as a personal affront. After all, wasn't she doing good? The child should be grateful! Aunt, in real life, belonged to that worthy sisterhood of charitable ladies who went about their business of doing good. "And not as easy as some people would think either!" For instance, some people accepted charity in the spirit in which it was given. The code was inviolate (the unwritten code of "Thank you" and a smile), but there were cases who took that smile for one of intimate friendship. Like that case last week when the woman had refused help for herself, but had got on her knees (terribly embarrassing) and had pleaded for help for her old mother and sister in some foreign country. These things didn't happen often, but when they did, she looked upon them as a personal failure. Of course *foreigners* had to be taught, but our own people should know better. The rules for accepting charity were simply to be thankful. Unlike this boy! She had done everything, everything possible to please him, but no. So she had thought of the ice cream.

Jack's eyes were still on Auntie's fingers.

The ice cream was sinking lower and lower, but still he wouldn't eat it. He was still clutching the spoon. One could see he was forced to a heavy discipline, a too heavy discipline possibly, but all the same his heart appeared to be fighting a heavy battle with his bottom lip.

Auntie sighed. Jack saw her looking at her wrist watch impatiently. But again her voice was sugared. "Eat, child, for goodness' sake! Don't you like ice cream?"

Jack felt the spoon getting heavier and heavier in his hand. Tears were stinging his eyelids. He could see the motor-cars behind Auntie's chair in a blur of shining colour. Everything was shining colour. He saw Aunt open her handbag and take out her hanky. She blew her nose and wiped her eyes. Kneading the bit of linen in her palm, she seemed to be murmuring to herself and sighing: "Well, I never! Not even the ice cream!" And then she was blowing her nose again and wiping her eyes.

Though Jack couldn't understand any of this, his fingers lost their cramp-like hold on the spoon. It dropped, falling on stone with a clatter which sent all the birds down there into a panic. They rose into the air, frightening all the other birds and suddenly the whole of that section of pavement was a thrash of wings. The air was full of feathers and while some people only waved their arms above their heads or hid their faces, others jumped up, spilling food and coffee into the laps.

A great big hand appeared before Jack's eyes. It whisked away the ice cream. In its place there was Aunt's furious face and the waiter's even more angrier expression. Aunt's cheeks turned red with embarrassment and she tried to apologise: "That's how the children are up there! God knows what will ever become of them, hooligans most likely!" The waiter agreed. He picked up the spoon, wiped it on his napkin and placed it on the table. In front of Jack. The ice cream was in his other hand.

"If he doesn't want it, he won't get it," said Auntie firmly, pulling herself together. People were looking at them. She felt a need to explain: "I've done all I could for this child. This is the ninth time I've brought him out. I took him to the zoo the first time. Then the park playground. Of course he wasn't allowed on the swings in his Sunday uniform but I thought it might give him pleasure to watch others play. I took him to the Museum and the Art Galleries, to give him an early sense of values. You just don't know what I haven't done for him! Like today, you saw for yourself how we've sat with this ice cream for over an hour." Her voice broke and again she sought her handkerchief. Her hands began to wrestle with each other in her lap. Like the animals he had seen at the zoo. Jack had been afraid of the animals. The way he was afraid of this "Auntie", knowing she was afraid of him. It had started on that first outing when Jack had tried to climb on Auntie's knee. His previous aunt had even cuddled him sometimes and sometimes even carried him when his legs got tired. Of course he had been a little boy then, almost a year ago, but Jack hadn't forgotten the way she had slapped him. Not hard, but firmly enough to remind him of his place.

"Come on! Time is up!" said Auntie suddenly, rising to her feet. Her voice was harsh and final. "Jack! Did you hear me?" The order was familiar to Jack, much more normal than the sweet voice which had never matched her eyes or movements. He jumped off the chair.

"Put your cap on."

Jack took his cap and put it on.

Auntie grabbed Jack's wrist with her bony fingers. The same fingers that had always given away her true feelings, that were like animals in the Zoo to the boy. He began to fight them and the harder he protested the more they bit deeper and deeper into his wrist. Those strawberry coloured lips opened, cream teeth grated. "You're making a public exhibition of yourself," she hissed. "I'm never bringing you out again as long as I live," and she shook him.

"...not bringing you out again"...was all Jack heard. The words were like apricot jam on fresh bread. His favourite food. Or like an ice cream...he stopped fighting.

Auntie hustled him away from the cafe and across the busy main road. He would have given anything to touch one of those motor-cars with his own hand. They passed a letter box and he wanted desperately to put his fingers in the slot and pretend to post a letter, to balance along the kerb or to jump the cracks in the paving stones, but he knew he couldn't, now. Still, the next Auntie might let him and what's more, she might even buy him an ice cream, a giant ice cream with strawberries and chocolate sauce, with yellow-white cream, and nuts and wafers that looked like two ears.

Jack allowed himself a skip and a jump and let Aunt press his fingers for the last time. It would be for the last time. They were almost home, hurrying towards the high wall. And both were feeling better.

Life
by Liam O'Flaherty

A poor peasant family in a country part of Ireland some years ago spans the whole of life.

The mother lay flat on her back, with her eyes closed and her arms stretched out to their full length above the bedclothes. Her hands kept turning back and forth in endless movement. Her whole body was exhausted after the great labour of giving birth.

Then the infant cried. She opened her eyes as soon as she heard the faint voice. She seized the bedclothes fiercely between her fingers. She raised her head and looked wildly towards the grandmother, who was tending the new-born child over by the fireplace.

The old woman noticed the mother's savage look. She burst out laughing.

"For the love of God," she said to the two neighbouring women that were helping her, "look at herself and she as frightened as a young girl on her wedding night. You'd think this is her first child instead of her last."

She took the infant by the feet, raised him up high and smacked him quite hard on the rump with her open palm.

"Shout now, in God's name," she said, "and put the devil out of your carcass."

The child started violently under the impact of the blow. He screamed again. Now there was power in his voice.

"Upon my soul!" said one of the neighbouring women. "I don't blame her at all for being conceited about a young fellow like that."

She spat upon the infant's naked stomach.

"I never laid eyes on a finer new-born son than this one, 'faith," she said in a tone of deep conviction.

"A fine lad, God bless him," said the other woman as she made the sign of the Cross over the child. "Begob, he has the makings of a hero in him, by all appearances."

"He has, indeed," said the grandmother. "He has the makings of a man in him, all right."

A deep sadness fell upon the mother when she heard the old woman say that this child would be the last to come from her womb. She was now forty-three. The years had already brought silver to her hair. She knew very well that she would never again bring life, by the miraculous power of God, from the substance of her body. She had done that

151

fourteen times already. Except for the first time, when the intoxication of love was still strong in her blood, she got little comfort from giving birth. As the holy seed of life multiplied under her roof, so also did misfortune and hunger multiply. It was so hard for a poor couple like her husband and herself, with only a few acres of stony land, to feed and care for so many little bodies and souls.

Yet she now felt miserably sad at the thought that her womb would henceforth be without fruit. She closed her eyes once more, crossed her hands on her bosom and began a prayer to Almighty God, asking for divine help on the hard road that lay ahead of her.

When the infant and the mother were put in order, the father was allowed to enter the bedroom. He was still in his prime, even though he was nearly fifty years of age, most of which time had been spent in drudgery on the land. He uncovered his head when he came into the presence of the new-born. He crossed himself and bent a knee in homage to the new life.

"May God bless you," he said to the child.

Then he went over to the bed and bowed to his wife in the same way.

"Thank God," he said to her gently, "you have that much past you."

She smiled faintly as she looked at him.

"I'm glad," she said, "that it was a son I gave you as my last child."

"May God reward you for it!" he said fervently as he again bowed to her.

The old woman brought the child to the bed and laid him against the mother's bosom.

"Here you are now," she said. "Here is the newest little jewel in your house."

All trace of sorrow departed from the mother's soul, as she put her hands about the infant's little body and felt the strong young heart beating behind the ribs. She got a lump in her throat and tears flowed down her cheeks.

"Praised be the great God of glory!" she cried fervently.

The cock began to crow out in the barn. Its voice rose

high and sharp above the roar of the November wind that was tearing through the sky.

"May the hand of God protect my child!" cried the mother when she heard the crowing of the cock.

All the village cocks kept joining in the crowing until they were of one voice saluting the dawn.

"May God preserve the little one!" said the other women.

Far away the sound of the waves was loud as they lashed the great southern cliffs.

"Safe from sickness," prayed the mother, "safe from blemish, safe from misfortune, safe in body and soul."

After a while, the other children were allowed to enter the room, so that they might make the acquaintance of their youngest little brother. There were seven of them. Four of the fourteen had already died. Another three had gone out into the world in search of a livelihood. All that remained were between the ages of fifteen and three. They became silent with wonder when they caught sight of the baby. They stood about the bed with their mouths open, holding one another by the hand.

Then the grandfather was allowed into the room. He was far from being silent. He began to babble foolishly when he caught sight of his youngest grandson.

"Aie! Aie!" he said. "Everything is more lasting than man. Aie! The Virgin Mary have pity on me! Look at me now and I only the wreck of a man. Yet there was a day . . ."

He was very old. A few years previously, the sun hurt him while he was asleep in a field on a warm day. He was practically a cripple since then, having lost the use of his limbs almost entirely. He was doting. His body shrank from day to day. Now he was no heavier than a little boy. His head was so stooped that one would think it was tethered to his ankles like that of a wicked ass. He trembled like a leaf.

"Aie! Aie!" he said bitterly. "There was a day when I wasn't afraid of any man, I don't care what man it was, from east or west, that might challenge me, looking for fight or for trouble. 'Faith, I'd let no man take the sway from me, for I was that sort of a man, that never looked for a fight and never ran from one. That was the class of a man I was, a man that could stand his ground without fear or favour..."

The old woman had to take hold of him and carry him out of the room.

"Come on down out of this," she said, "and don't be bothering the people with your foolish talk."

"Ah! God help me!" said one of the neighbouring women. "The longest journey from the womb to the grave is only a short one after all."

When the baby took up residence in his cradle by the kitchen hearth, he was like a king in the house. The whole family waited on him. It was thankless work. The new-born was entirely unaware that the slightest favour was being conferred on him. He was completely unaware of all but the solitary instinct that he had brought with him from the womb. That was to maintain and strengthen the life that was in him.

When he awoke, he screamed savagely until he was given hold of his mother's breast. Then he became silent at once. His toothless jaws closed firmly on the swollen teat. His little body shivered with voluptuous pleasure when he felt the first stream of warm milk pouring on to his tongue. He sucked until he was replete. Then again he fell asleep. When he felt unwell, from stomach-ache or some other trivial complaint, he yelled outrageously. He went on yelling in most barbarous fashion until they began to rock the cradle. They had to keep rocking until his pain had gone.

They sang to him while they rocked.

"Oh! My darling! My darling! My darling!" they sang to him. "Oh! My darling, you're the love of my heart."

Far different was their conduct towards the old man. There was little respect for him. When they waited on him, it was through charity and not because it gave them pleasure. They begrudged him the smallest favour that they conferred on him.

"Look at that old devil," they used to say. "Neither God

nor man can get any good out of him and he sitting there in the chimney corner from morning till night. You'd be better off begging your bread than waiting on him."

True enough, it was hard to blame them for complaining. It was very unpleasant work having to wait upon the poor old man. They had to take him from his sleeping place each morning. They had to clean and dress him and put him seated on a little stool in the chimney corner. They had to tie a horse-hair rope around his waist, lest he might fall into the fire. At mealtimes, they had to mash his food and put it in his mouth with a spoon.

He was dependent on them in every way exactly like the infant.

"Aie! The filthy thing!" they used to say. "It would be a great kindness to the people of this house if God would call him."

The grandfather remained tied in his chimney corner all day, between sleep and wake, jabbering, threatening imaginary people with his stick, scolding enemies that were long since dead, making idiotic conversation with the creatures of his folly about people and places.

He only emerged from his witless state when he heard the infant cry on awaking from sleep.

"Who is this?" he would say with his ear cocked. "Who is squealing like this?"

When the mother took the baby from the cradle and gave it suck in the opposite corner, the old man's eyes would brighten and he would recognise the child.

"Ho! Ho!" he would cry in delight. "It's yourself that's in it. Ho! My lovely one! That's a pretty young man I see over opposite me and no doubt about it."

Then he would try to reach the infant. He would get angry when he failed to go farther than the length of his horse-hair rope.

"Let me at him," he would cry, struggling to leave his stool. "Let go this rope, you pack of devils. He is over there, one of my kindred. Let me at him. He is a man of my blood. Let me go to him."

His rage never lasted long. He would get overcome with

delight on seeing the infant stretch and shudder voluptuously as he sucked.

"Bravo! Little one," the old man then cried as he jumped up and down on his stool. "Throw it back, my boy. Don't leave a drop of it. Ho! You are a man of my blood, all right. Drink, little one. More power to you!"

Winter was almost spent before the infant recognised anybody. Until then he only knew his mother's breasts and the warmth of his cradle by means of touch. Even though he often watched what was happening about him, there was no understanding in his big staring blue eyes. Then the day came at last when the resplendent soul shone out through his eyes.

He was lying on his belly across his mother's lap, suffering a little from stomach-ache owing to having drunk too much, when he took note of the old man's foolish gestures in the opposite corner. He smiled at first. Then he began to clap hands and to leap exactly like the old man. He uttered a little jovial yell.

"Praised be the great God of Glory!" said the mother.

The household gathered round. They all stood looking at the infant and at the old man, who were imitating one another's foolish gestures across the hearth. Everybody laughed gaily except the grandmother. It was now she began to weep out loud.

"Aie! My Lord God!" she wailed. "The foolishness of infancy is a lovely thing to behold, but it's pitiful to see an old person that has outlived his reason."

From that day onward, the old man and the baby spent long spells playing together, clapping hands, jabbering and drivelling. It would be hard to say which of them was the more foolish. When the infant was weaned, it was with the same mash they were both fed.

According as the infant grew strong from day to day the old man weakened. He got bronchitis in spring and they thought that his end had come. He received Extreme Unction[1]. Yet he recovered from that attack. He was soon

1 *Extreme Unction:* the last sacrament of the Christian Church for those at the point of death.

able to leave his bed and resume his position in the hearth corner. Now he was merely a shadow of his former self. They could lift him with one hand.

A day came early in May when there was a big spring tide and the whole family went to pick carrigeen moss along the shore. The grandmother was left to take care of the house, the infant and the old man. It was a fine sunny day.

"Take me out into the yard," the old man said to his wife. "I'd like to see the sun before I die."

She did as he asked her. She put him sitting in a straw chair outside the door. She herself sat on a stool near him, with the infant on her bosom. She began to call the fowls.

"Tiuc! Tiuc!" she cried. "Fit! Fit! Beadai! Beadai!"

They all came running to her at top speed, hens and ducks and geese. She threw them scraps of food from a big dish. The birds began to fight for the food, as they leaped and screamed and prodded one another with their beaks.

The infant took delight in the tumult of the birds. He began to clap his hands and to leap, as he watched the fierce struggle of the winged creatures. He screamed with glee in answer to their harsh croaking.

"Ho! Ho! Ho!" he cried, while the spittle ran from his mouth.

The old man got equally excited and he imitated the gestures of the infant. He began to clap hands and to hop on his chair and to babble unintelligibly.

"Musha, God help the two of you!" the old woman said.

The old man became silent all of a sudden. She glanced anxiously in his direction. She saw him half erect and leaning forward. Then he fell to the ground head foremost. She rushed to him with the child under her arm. When she stooped over him, she heard the death rattle in his throat. Then there was nothing at all to be heard from him.

She stood up straight and began the lamentation for the newly dead.

"Och! Ochon!" she wailed. "It was with you I walked through the delight and sorrow of life. Now you are gone and I'll soon be following you. Och! Ochon! My love! It was you that was lovely on the day of our marriage..."

When the neighbours came, the old woman sat lamenting on her stool by the corpse with the child within her arms, while the birds still leaped and fought savagely for the food in the dish.

The infant hopped up and down, shouting merrily as he struggled to touch the bright feathers of the rushing birds with his outstretched hands.

The strong young heart was unaware that the tired old heart had just delivered up the life that made it beat.

Points for Discussion

The Life Guard

1 What sort of a person is Hopper?
2 Why is Jimmy so desperate to keep his job?
3 How does Jimmy feel by the end of the story?
4 Which of the main characters do you consider most to blame?

A & P

1 Do you think the girls were deliberately trying to make a stir?
2 Who acted more sensibly—the manager or Sammy?
3 Will Sammy regret what he has done later?

A Woman on a Roof

1 In what ways are the three men's reactions different?
2 Do you think Tom was stupid to do as he did?

First Kiss

1 What are the young man's various reasons for wanting to kiss Claire?
2 What do you think the future of their relationship is likely to be?

Ellen

1 Ought old Mr Mason to have given any different advice to Ellen?
2 Do *you* think that Joe will come back? Explain your reasons.

The Green Hills

1 What would you have done if you were Martha at the beginning of the story?
2 Why does the story end with the mention of "the green hills" of the title?

Their Mother's Purse

1 What is the difference between the parents' attitude to Joe and to Mary?
2 How do you think Joe and Mary will behave towards each other after this incident?

The Road

1 What kinds of things do Amy and Stanley disagree about? Why do you think they disagree so much?
2 What memories of the day do you think Ivan had? Amy asked Stanley "What effect do you think all this arguing and fighting's going to have on him?" What do *you* think?

The Berry Holly

1 Why do you think the mother and father parted?
2 Do you consider the family will be happy now? Explain your reasons.
3 *Was* he "a fortunate child"?

Fire

1 What is the mood of the two young men as they go to their homes?
2 How does the young man feel towards his mother before and after the accident?

The Sniper

1 Do you think the sniper has any feelings, or is he just coldly carrying out a job?
2 Is his discovery at the end of the story likely to make him give up his part in the fighting?

The Case for the Defence

1 In what ways did Mrs Salmon seem a convincing witness?
2 Do you consider that such an event could really take place?

The Killers

1 What sort of a person is George?
2 How could it be that Ole Andreson is apparently so *accepting* of his likely death?

Hallmarked

1 Before you found out about Paul's past, why did you think he had come to this village?
2 What is life like for Michael John and the people in the village?
3 What picture did you get of the commercial traveller who arrives near the end? Could he have acted any differently?

Twenty Pieces of Silver

1 What were the differences between Mrs Fosdyke and Mrs Marsden?
2 Why do you think Mrs Marsden left the £1 note in the suit?
3 Do you think that the younger Miss Norris was right when she said to Mrs Fosdyke: "You're such a *good* collector. Everybody gives so generously when you go

round." (p. 143)? If so, why do you think this is?

4 What is your impression of the sisters?

The Ice Cream

1 Why is Jack's "Aunt" so cross?
2 At the end of the story it says: "And both were feeling better" (p. 149). Why were they feeling better?

Life

1 The family in this story lives in very different ways from the families we know. Compare this life with family life today. Does this Irish family have any advantages that we lack?
2 Compare the difference between the way the baby and the old man are treated. Is this difference in any way typical of life in general?
3 Do you find this a happy story or a sad one? (Explain your reasons in as much detail as possible.)

Ideas for Writing

The Life Guard

1 Write a report of the drowning for the Red Rocks local newspaper.
2 Describe Jimmy's feelings and thoughts the next day.

A & P

1 Write the conversations in which (a) Sammy and (b) the Manager tell their families of the afternoon's event.
2 Describe a situation in which you have stood up against the person in charge to defend someone else.

A Woman on a Roof

Write a story about Tom at some other point in his life.

First Kiss

Write another story about different people, with the same title.

Ellen

Describe the situation from Joe's point of view.

The Green Hills

Write a story or a poem called "Parting".

Their Mother's Purse

1 Describe the next meeting between Mary & Joe.
2 Write an imaginary letter from Mary to her secret husband, Paul, in the sanatorium.

The Road

1 Write about another argument between Amy and Stanley.
2 Describe what Ivan did between leaving Stanley and being found on the church steps.
3 Write a short story based on any family argument which you have seen.

The Berry Holly

1 Imagine the last meeting of the mother and father before this story took place.
2 Describe the Christmas after this meeting has happened.

Fire

1 Describe the scene from the mother's point of view.
2 Write about any accident at home that you have been involved in.

The Sniper

1 Write a story based on some more recent fighting.
2 Describe what you think the Sniper would do next.

The Case for the Defence

1 Write a short story in which some years later Mrs Salmon thinks she sees the man again and is frightened.
2 Write the report which the narrator of the story might have sent to his newspaper.

The Killers

1 This story is written almost entirely in dialogue, with only a little description. Write about another encounter in a similar "lunch-counter" that Nick Adams might have seen.
2 Imagine and describe what eventually happened to Ole Andreson.

Hallmarked

1 Write the next episode in "Paul's" life. Where could he go next, and what could he do?
2 Imagine another, completely different, situation in which someone finds themselves "hallmarked" and recognised from the past. Write a story based on your idea, and also called "Hallmarked".

Twenty Pieces of Silver

1 Write a description of Mrs Fosdyke's return home on the day she was accused of stealing the money, and include the conversation she had with her husband.
2 Imagine and write the conversation of the two Misses Norris on their way home.

The Ice Cream

1 Write the letter which Jack's "Aunt" might send to the Principal of the home to explain why she will not be able to see him again.
2 Write Jack's description of the afternoon as he might have given it on returning to his friends at the "Home".
3 Describe an occasion, if there has been one, when someone has tried to be generous to you, but the occasion has gone wrong.

Life

1 Write a poem or a story of your own with this title.
2 Write another episode in the life of this family.

To the Teacher

Amongst all the difficulties of secondary education, one of the major successes in the years since the Newsom report, say, has been the involvement of older pupils of all abilities with a range of good contemporary literature. The short story, as I have argued in my *Towards the New Fifth* (Longman, 1969), has contributed especially to this success. This volume has grown out of the extensive experience of planning and using the first twenty-five volumes of the *Longman Imprint Books*. Most of the volumes can be used with a very wide range of pupils, but the needs of those who find reading difficult have been the special concern of this collection.

I have aimed to produce a book with a large number of mostly very short stories, which have both some common points of interest and related themes, and yet at the same time have a wide range of setting, types of characters, and moods. Strength of theme and simplicity of approach and form have been the twin aims, but I have been determined that in the search for simplicity and strength of appeal the tradition of reading good writing should be maintained. The range of authors is extremely wide, including such major figures as Hemingway and Graham Greene, as well as a number of the best contemporary masters of the short story from America, Ireland, and Britain. In each case the story chosen seems to me a good example of the writer's art, both in the well known and in the more recent or less well known. It is amazing how many very good short stories have been written in this century, and more particularly since the last war. In searching for the seventeen in this collection I have had to put to one side very many which I judged to be too difficult in conception, too complicated in language, too remote in theme, or just too long for the needs of this book. I hope that the seventeen with which I have finished up will contribute to purposeful reading and writing with older pupils. The loves, hopes, and fears of these characters seem to me to echo in the mind long after the story has been put down.

M.M.

A choice of books

In reading, one title leads on to another, and we often find most pleasure in picking up a book which in some way or other has been prompted by what we have just read and enjoyed. Listed here is a small choice of books which in various ways touch on similar experiences and ideas to those of the stories in this collection. It would be especially good for members of a group working with this collection each to read a different book from this list and to compare notes later.

Stories

BANKS, LYNN REID, *The L-Shaped Room,* Longman (*Imprint Books*)

BARSTOW, STAN, *A Kind of Loving,* Hutchinson

BARSTOW, STAN, *Joby,* Bodley Head

BARSTOW, STAN, *Watchers on the Shore,* Bodley Head

BARSTOW, STAN, *The Human Element,* Longman (*Imprint Books*)

BATES, H.E, *The Good Corn and other stories,* Longman (*Imprint Books*)

BEHAN, BRENDAN, *Borstal Boy,* Hutchinson

CALLOW, PHILIP, *Going to the Moon,* MacGibbon & Kee

CALLOW, PHILIP, *Native Ground,* Heinemann

CHAPLIN, SID, *The Leaping Lad,* Longman (*Imprint Books*)

DAVIES, MARILYN, AND MARLAND, MICHAEL, editors, *Breaking Away,* Longman (*Imprint Books*)

DRABBLE, MARGARET, *The Millstone,* Longman (*Imprint Books*)

DYMENT, CLIFFORD, *The Railway Game,* Dent

FOSTER, JOHN, editor, *The Experience of Sport,* Longman (*Imprint Books*)

GREENE, GRAHAM, *Stories,* Bodley Head and Penguin

GREENE, GRAHAM, *Brighton Rock,* Heinemann Educational Books

HANLEY, CLIFFORD, *A Taste of Too Much,* Blackie

HEMINGWAY, ERNEST, *A Hemingway Selection,* Longman (*Imprint Books*)

HEMINGWAY, ERNEST, *A Farewell to Arms,* Jonathan Cape

KAMM, JOSEPHINE, *Young Mother,* Heinemann

LESSING, DORIS, *The Grass is Singing,* Heinemann Educational Books

LESSING, DORIS, *Nine African Stories,* Longman (*Imprint Books*)

MACKEN, WALTER, *God Made Sunday and other Stories,* Macmillan

MARLAND, EILEEN and MICHAEL, editors, *Friends and Families,* Longman (*Imprint Books*)

MARLAND, MICHAEL, editor, *The Experience of Work,* Longman (*Imprint Books*)

MOODY, H.L.B., *Facing Facts,* Blackie

NAUGHTON, BILL, *Late Night on Watling Street,* Longman (*Imprint Books*)

ROWE, ALBERT, *People Like You,* Faber

SILLITOE, ALAN, *A Sillitoe Selection,* Longman (*Imprint Books*)

SILLITOE, ALAN, *The Loneliness of the Long-Distance Runner,* Longman (*Heritage of Literature Series*)

SMITH, C.E.J., editor, *Ten Western Stories,* Longman (*Imprint Books*)

UNWIN, G.G., editor, *A Taste for Living,* Faber

WATERHOUSE, KEITH, *There is a Happy Land,* Longman (*Imprint Books*)

WRIGHT, RICHARD, *Black Boy,* Longman (*Imprint Books*)

Plays

BARSTOW, STAN, and BRADLEY, ALFRED, *A Kind of Loving*, Blackie

DELANEY, SHELAGH, *A Taste of Honey*, Methuen

MARLAND, MICHAEL, editor, *Theatre Choice*, Blackie

RECKFORD, BARRY, *Skyvers*, Penguin

TERSON, PETER, *Zigger-Zagger*, Penguin

WATERHOUSE, KEITH and HALL, WILLIS, *Billy Liar*, Blackie

Acknowledgements

We are grateful to the following for permission to reproduce copyright material: Author's Agents for 'The Life Guard' from *The Life Guard and Other Stories* by John Wain and for 'A Woman On A Roof' from *A Man and Two Women* by Doris Lessing; Jonathan Cape Ltd. and Charles Scribner's Sons for 'The Killers' from *Men Without Women* by Ernest Hemingway. Copyright 1927 Charles Scribner's Sons. Reprinted by permission of Charles Scribner's Sons and the Executors of the Ernest Hemingway Estate; Jonathan Cape Ltd. for 'The Sniper' from *The Short Stories of Liam O'Flaherty* by Liam O'Flaherty; Andre Deutsch Ltd. for 'A. & P.' from *Pigeon Feathers and Other Stories* by John Updike. Published by Andre Deutsch Ltd; Author's Agents for 'Twenty Pieces of Silver' from *A Season with Eros* by Stan Barstow; Granada Publishing Ltd. for 'Ellen' and 'Their Mother's Purse' from *Short Stories* by Morley Callagham; Author's Agents for *The Berry Holly* by Sid Chaplin. Published by Longman Group Ltd; Author's Agents for 'First Kiss' and 'Fire' from *Native Ground* by Philip Callow. (c) Philip Callow 1959. Reprinted by permission of John Johnson; Macmillan (Basingstoke) Ltd. for 'The Road' from *Guzman Go Home And Other Stories* by Alan Sillitoe. Reprinted by permission of Macmillan London and Basingstoke and for 'The Green Hills' and 'Hallmarked' from *The Green Hills and Other Stories* by Walter Macken. Reprinted by permission of Macmillan, London and Basingstoke; Author's Agents for 'Life' from *Two Lovely Beasts and Other Stories* by Liam O'Flaherty. Reprinted by permission of A.D. Peters and Company and Author's Agents for 'The Case for the Defence' from *Collected Stories* by Graham Greene. Published by The Bodley Head and William Heinemann Ltd.

We regret we have been unable to trace the copyright holder of the story 'The Ice Cream' by Elin Toona from BBC Broadcast 22nd January, 1967.

Lance Brown for the photographs throughout the book.